international thai cooking

SPICY THAI CUISINE

SD BOOKS

Sangdad Books

National Library of Thailand Cataloging in Publication Data
SPICY THAI CUISINE.--4th ed.--Bangkok : Sangdad, 2004.
  104 p.
  1. Cookery, Thai. I. Title.
641.59593
ISBN : 974-7162-05-9

SPICY THAI CUISINE

First Published, May 1996
Second Published, January 2000
Third Published, January 2002
Fourth Published, July 2004
Copyright © 1996, 2000, 2002, 2004 by Sangdad Publishing Co., Ltd.
Photography Copyright © 1996, 2000, 2002, 2004 by Sangdad Publishing Co., Ltd.

Consultant	Sisamon Kongpan
Director	Nidda Hongwiwat
Editor	Nalin Khu-Armornpatana
English Editor	Richard Goldrick
Editor's Assistant	Obchoel Imsabai
Photography & Design	Samart Sudto
Layout	Rungrudee Panichsri
Marketing Director	Nan Hongvivatana
	e-mail : marketing@sangdad.com
Production Director	Jiranan Tubniem
	e-mail : production@sangdad.com
Printer	Pimdee Co., Ltd.
	Tel. (662) 803-2694-7

Published and Distributed by Sangdad Publishing Co., Ltd.
320 Lat Phrao 94 (Town in Town) Wangthonglang, Bangkok 10310, Thailand.
Tel. (662) 934-4413, 934-4418-20 ext. 101
Fax. (662) 538-1499
www.sangdad.com
e-mail : sdbooks@sangdad.com

PREFACE

*Hot and spicy, the distinguished
taste of Thai Cuisine.*

Traditional Thai cuisine has various dishes of hot and spicy food. They are stir-fried dishes, hot and sour soups, and especially spicy and sour salads or *yam* dishes. Furthermore, there is a wide range of chilli sauce served with several kinds of vegetables and fish. This cook book focuses on two dishes; *yam* and *tom yam* (hot and sour soup).

Hot and spicy food is normally on the table of every meal in Thai house, particularly at dinner, the biggest meal of day. The most popular dish is *yam* because of its simplicity of cooking and flexibility of mixtures. Even in a party, *yam* is served. The taste of *yam* is the blending of four basic flavors: sour, salty, sweet and hot or pungent, the distinguished taste of Thai cuisine. By blending these flavors in varying proportions, a racy dish with harmony of taste can be achieved.

Hot and sour soup or *tom yam* is another vigorous dish. Its flavor is a delightful combination of four main taste: hot, sour, sweet and salty, with the fresh aroma of spice and herb: lemongrass, kaffir lime leaf, galangal, etc.

Apart form their magnificent taste, *yam* and *tom yam* are the perfect dishes for those who are health conscious. They contain little fat and low calories but high nutritional value. Above all, they are easy to make.

Nidda Hongwiwat
Managing Director

INTRODUCTION

The taste fo Thai hot and spicy dishes mainly depends on the freshness of ingredients and the harmonious blending of poignant flavors: hot and sour, with subtle sweet and salty. Varying their mixtures will introduce new surprisingly different results.

The describtions of various ingredients will guide you to the right and suitable way to prepare each mixture.

SEAFOOD

Prawn

The **white prawn,** kung chae-buai,กุ้งแชบ๊วย, also called the banana prawn, has a white body stippled with minute dots of rust-colored pigment. Fully grown, these prawns attain a length of 20 cm. and more; however, harvesting may begin before they have reached half this. These smaller ones, sorted and priced by size, are sold as kung chihae, กุ้งชีแฮ้, which in the recipes are designated simply as prawns.

Tiger prawn, kung kula dam,กุ้งกุลาดำ, so called because of its black and white stripes, is the giant among Asian prawns, the females growing to over 30 cm. long. Pond rearing of tiger prawns was more recently established than that of the white prawn but is very promising.

Squid

The **squid,** *Loligo formosana,* called pla meuk kluai, **ปลาหมึกกล้วย,** has a tubular boby with fins at one end and tentacles at the other. The body is covered with a thin skin flecked with red. Afte washing, this is removed and the separated tentacles and head are clear bone from the body. The membrane, which and associated are attached to the head, are discarded. Then, the eyes and ink sac are cut away, the hard beak is removed, and the squid is washed again.

Cuttlefish

The **cuttlefish,** *Sepia pharonis,* called pla meuk kradong, **ปลาหมึกกระดอง,** has a flattened, broad, white body. After washing, the head and tentacles are slipped away from the body, the cuttlebone and the membranes around it are removed, and the preparation continues like that of the squid. It is customary to score it in a criss-cross pattern.

Jellyfish

The **jellyfish,** maeng ka-phrun, **แมงกะพรุน,** is sold in dried form. It is something of a specialty product, so go to one of the bigger markets to look for it.

Cockles, Mussels, and Clams

The **scallop,** *Amusium pleuronectes,* called hoi chen, **หอยเชลล์,** and also hoi phat,**หอยพัด.**

The **cockle,** *Anadara granosa* and A. *nodifera,* called hoi khraeng, **หอยแครง,** in Thai and also known in English as the ark shell and as the blood cockle, has a thick, highly arched shell with ridges radiating from the hinge. The shell, 5-6 cm. long, is white near the hinge and brown near the opposite margin.

The **clam** which is most readily available in the market is the undulated surf clam, *Paphia undulata*, called hoi lai, หอยลาย. The shell is covered with a pleasing pattern of branching lines and grows 5-6 cm. long.

The **mussel**, *Perna viridis*, called hoi malaeng phu, หอยแมลงภู่, has a dark brown shell which is green at the margin and reaches a length of 20 cm.

Fish

Sea perch, pla kaphong, ปลากะพง, is a general name for fish of the sea bass and sea perch families.

Serpent head, pla chon, ปลาช่อน, is the freshwater fish *Ophiocephalus striatus*.

HERBS AND SPICES

Green pepper, phrik-thai-awn, พริกไทยอ่อน, is almost mature pepper berries which are pruned form the vines in thinning so that the remaining berries can develop fully. When nearly ripe pepper corns are dried in the sun, they are called black pepper, and when fully matured corns are sun dried, they take on a whitish color, and so are called white pepper. Black pepper is not so hot as white pepper, and so green pepper is not very hot.

Green pepper is used in curries made without coconut milk, in Thai-style stir-fried

dishes, and in chilli sauces. If kept long, green pepper will go bad, so it is usually not washed. If it is washed, it should be dried and then placed in a container in the refrigerator. Green pepper is not as fragrant as dried pepper.

Pepper, phrik thai, พริกไทย, *Piper nigrum*, produces berries, which, when ripe, are dried and ground with the skins on to give black pepper, or with the skins off to give white pepper. The most widely available form in Thailand is white peper.

Dried chilli, phrik haeng, พริกแห้ง, is fully ripened, red spur chillies dried either in the sun or by smoking. They may be large or small, depending on the variety of spur chilli used. They are prepared by removing the seeds, soaking in water, and then pounding in a mortar. Bright red dried chillies should be selected for the color they lend chilli pastes. Smoked chillies are darker in color.

Shallot, hom lek, หอมเล็ก, or hom daeng, หอมแดง, *Allium ascalonicum*, is the zesty small red onion flavored in Thai cooking.

Garlic, kra-thiam, กระเทียม, *Allium sativum*, Thai garlic has small cloves covered with a peel that is not tough. Its fragrance is stronger than that of large cloved garlic. In making fried garlic, the peel is usually not removed entirely so that only the flesh re- mains. Some of the peel is left on the clove, for it is in the peel that the fragrance resides.

Galangal, kha, ข่า, *Alpinia galangal,* is a largar and lighter-colored relative of ginger and has its own distinctive taste.

Lemon grass, ta-khrai, ตะไคร้, *Cymbopgon citratus,* is an aromatic grey-green grass. The bases of the stems are used in cookery.

Kaffir lime, ma-kruut, มะกรูด, *Citrus hystrix.* The had green fruits with wrinkled skin. rind and the leaves are used in cookery.

Ginger, khing, ขิง, *Zingiber officinale,* grows from an un- derground stem, or rhisome. Mature ginger stems are buff colored; young or fresh ginger, khing on, ขิงอ่อน, is white and is eaten fresh, and pickled as well as cooked.

Mint leaves, sa-ra-nae, สะระแหน่. Thai mint leaves, are round, not thick, hair- less, and slightly wavy. The stem tends to be dark red. It is easy to grow, and Thai commonly plant it in pots kept near the kitchen, where it can always be easily gathered.

FRUITS AND VEGETABLES

Cucumber, taeng kwa, แตงกวา, *Cucumis sativus,* has short fruits about 8 cm. long which are crispiest while still green and white, before yellowing. A larger type, taeng ran, แตงร้าน, are alsoeaten.

Celery, kheun chai, ขึ้นฉ่าย, *Apium graveolens,* also called celeriae, turniprooted celery, or Chinese soup celery, has very small stalks (only a few millimeters across) and a very strong flavor.

Coriander, phak chi, ผักชี, *Coriandrum sativum,* is of the parsley family. The leaves and stems are eaten fresh and used frequently as a garnish. The root and the seeds are ingerdients in many dishes. The root is taken from the fresh plant. The seeds which are roughly spherical, 2-4 cm. in dia- meter, and range in color from off-white to brown, have a pleasant taste and fragrance. They can be bought in the market. It is better to roast and grind seeds im- mediately.

Kale, phak kha-na, ผัก *oleracea* คะน้า, *Brassica* (acephala variety),

has leathery grey-green leaves on thick stalks. Stalk lovers buy the large variety, while those partial to the leaves get the dwarf variety.

Bitter gourd, ma-ra, มะระ, *Momordica charantia,* also called bitter cucumber, carilla fruit, or balsam pear, is an oblong fruit, pointed at one end, which has a handsome pale green surface covered with an irregular pattern of ridges. There are also small dark green varieties. The young leaves and shoots are also eaten. All are bitter to the taste.

Spur chilli, phrik chi fa, พริกชี้ฟ้า, have plump lang-like fruits 7-12 cm. long. The green immature fruits become red, orange, or yellow when ripe. Hot.

Bell chilli, phrik yuak, พริกหยวก, is light green in color and mild in taste. They are used in spicy salads and chilli pastes for their fragrance, and in stir-fried meat dishes for both flavor and aroma.

Hot chilli, phrik khinu, พริกขี้หนู, are the hottest type and also the smallest, being only about a centimeter long.

Lime, ma-nao, มะนาว, *Citrus acide,* has small, spherical fruits which are usually green but some are yellow. The rind is thin. The juice is an important ingredient in many dishes. Lemon juice is a substitute.

Papaya, malakor, มะละกอ, a large green gourd-like fruit with soft yellow-orange flesh. When unripe and still green the fresh is used as vegetable.

Coconut, ma-phrao, มะพร้าว, *Cocos nucifera,* is found nearly everywhere people have settled in all parts of the country and its production is important to the economy. The use of coconut milk in curries is a hallmark of Thai cooking. The meat of ripe nuts is scraped either by hand or by machine. The grated coconut is placed in a basin and mixed with a certain amount of warm water. The coconut is then picked up in the hand, held over a second container, and squeezed to press out the **coconut milk,** ka-thi, กะทิ, A fine-meshed strainer should be positioned below the hand during squeezing to catch any meat that falls. Many cooks add a little salt to the water or the milk.

Coconut cream, hua ka-thi,หัวกะทิ, can be obtained by mixing a little warm water with the grated coconut and collecting the required amount of cream on the first squeezing.

Following this, water can be addded again and the grated coconut can be squeezed a second and a third time to obtain a less rich milk, which is kept separate from the cream. Alternatively, the full amount of warm water may be mixed with the grated coconut. After squeezing, the liquid is allowed to stand for a time, and then the cream is skimmed from top with a spoon.

Fastidious cooks scrape mature brown coconuts themselves by hand and coconut thus grated is usually pure white. In the market, however, the work is done with a machine that accepts chunks of coconut cut from the shell and usually a thin layer of shell still adheres to the meat. As a result, the grated coconut sold in the market is flecked with tiny brown particles of shell. This is useable for making coconut milk but is unacceptable when the grated coconut itself is to be used, for example, as a topping for a sweet. For such purposes, the recipes specify **white grated coconut**, ma-phrao khao, มะพร้าวขาว, which is also available in the market.

Ripe tamarind, ma-kham piak, มะขามเปียก, is the flesh, seeds, and veins, of several fruit pressed together in the hand to form a wad.

Tamarind juice, nam ma-kham piak, น้ำ-มะขามเปียก, is obtained by mixing some of the ripe fruit with water and squeezing out the juice. The immature fruit and the young leaves and flowers are also used, all to give a sour taste. There are also sweet tamarinds which are a delight to eat and command a high price.

Pomelo, som-o, ส้มโอ, the largest of the citrus fruits, is native to Southeast Asia and Thailand. There are many varieties with different taste. Some tastes sweet and fragrance. Some is sweet with sour tang. It is a popular fruit and often used in Thai cuisine to counteract the flavour of hot and spicy dishes, such as *yam*. The pomelo for *yam* dishes should be fully ripe with sweet and sour taste.

Water lilly stem, sai-bua, สายบัว, a long thin stem of lotus is used as a kind of vegetable in Thailand. You can eat it fresh in *yam* dish or cook it, like *tom sai-bua platu sod* (water lilly stem boiled with mackerel). Its outer layer should be peeled off before cooking.

SAUCE

Fish sause, nam pla, น้ำปลา, is a clear, brown liquid derived from a brew of fish or shrimp mixed with salt. It is sold in bottles and plastic jugs as well as in earthenware jars. High quality fish sauce has a fine aroma and taste. Fish sauce is placed on the table as a condiment at nearly every meal, either as is or mixed with sliced chillies and perhaps lime juice.

Palm sugar, nam tan pip, น้ำตาลปีบ, was originally made from the sap of the sugar, or palmyra, palm, *Borassus flabellifera*, called tan in Thai, which has a very rough trunk and large, fan-shapped leaves. Now it is generally made from the sap of coconut plams, and may be sold as coconut  sugar. The sugar is a light golden brown paste with a distinctive flavor and fragrance. It is put up in five-gallon kerosene cans, called pip in Thai.

Roasted chilli sauce, nam phrik phao, น้ำพริกเผา, is a mixture of chillies, garlic, dried shrimp, and palm sugar which is stir fried until fragrant. It can be bought in markets and supermarkets or can be made at home. It can be spread on bread, mixed with rice.

CONTENTS

58 PLA MEUK NEUNG MA-NAO
Steamed squid with lime sauce

60 KUNG NEUNG RAT PHRIK MA-NAO
Steamed prawns with chilli and lime sauce

62 MU MA-NAO
Boiled pork with lime sauce

64 YAM TAENG
Spicy shredded cucumber salad

66 KUNG NEUNG KHAI ROD SEAP
Spicy and sour steamed egg

68 PLA CHAWN YANG SEAP
Northeastern-style broiled serpent-head fish

70 YAM PHRIK WAN
Spicy sweet pepper salad

72 PHLA PLA KROB
Spicy roasted fish salad

74 YAM PHRIK CHI FA
Spicy spur chilli salad

76 SOM TAM MALAKOR
Papaya salad

78 YAM PLA THU KAP SAI BUA
Spicy mackerel and water lily stem salad

80 YAM PHRIK YUAK
Spicy bell chilli salad

82 YAM PLA CHAWN KROB
Spicy fried serpent-fish salad

84 YAM NEUA ROD DED
Spicy broiled beef salad

86 PHLA NEUA MA-KHEUA PRAW
Broiled beef and eggplant spicy salad

88 TAP WAN
Savory liver

90 TOM YAM PLA CHAWN
Sour and spicy serpent-head fish soup

92 TOM YAM KHAI PLA
Sour and spicy fish roe soup

94 TOM YAM PLA KAO THOD KROB
Sour and spicy crisp grouper soup

96 TOM YAM KHA MU
Sour and spicy fresh pork hock soup

98 TOM PRIAO
Sour fish soup

100 TOM YAM HUA PLA NAM SAI
Clear spicy fish head soup

102 KEANG SOM PLA CHAWN KROB
Sour tamarind soup with fried serpent-head fish

YAM KUNG
Spicy prawn salad
ยำกุ้ง

INGREDIENTS

300	grams white prawns
4	thinly sliced shallots
1	tbsp. finely sliced lemon grass
1	tbsp. shredded young ginger
9	crushed hot chillies
2 1/2	tbsp. lime juice
1	tbsp. fish sauce
1	tbsp. roasted chilli paste

Fresh vegetables : mint leaves, lettuce, spring shallots

PREPARATION

1. Wash, shell, and vein the prawns. Spoon into boiling water. When done, remove from water and drain.

2. Mix the shallot, ginger, chillies, roasted chilli paste, lime juice, and fish sauce together; then, add the prawns and stir. Add the lemon grass and mix gently.

3. Transfer onto a serving dish, serve with fresh vegetables.

เครื่องปรุง

กุ้งแชบ๊วย 300 กรัม
หอมแดงซอย 4 หัว
ตะไคร้ซอย 1 ช้อนโต๊ะ
ขิงอ่อนซอย 1 ช้อนโต๊ะ
พริกขี้หนูบุบ 9 เม็ด
น้ำมะนาว 2 1/2 ช้อนโต๊ะ
น้ำปลา 1 ช้อนโต๊ะ
น้ำพริกเผา 1 ช้อนโต๊ะ
ผักสด : สะระแหน่ ผักกาดหอม ต้นหอม

วิธีทำ

1. ล้างกุ้ง แกะเปลือกผ่าหลังชักเส้นดำออก ตั้งน้ำ ให้เดือด ลวกกุ้งพอสุก ตักขึ้นให้สะเด็ดน้ำ

2. ผสมหอมแดง ขิง พริกขี้หนู น้ำพริกเผา น้ำ-มะนาว น้ำปลา เข้าด้วยกัน เคล้าส่วนผสมกับกุ้ง เข้าด้วยกัน ใส่ตะไคร้ คลุกเบา ๆพอทั่ว

3. ตักใส่จาน เสิร์ฟพร้อมผักสด

YAM PLA MEUK
Squid spicy salad
ยำปลาหมึก

INGREDIENTS

500 grams squid
1/2 cup thinly sliced young ginger
1 onion, cut into thin slices
1 cup short lengths of Chinese celery
1/4 cup mint leaves
1 thinly sliced red spur chilli

DRESSING INGREDIENTS

10 tiny hot chillies, finely pounded
3 garlic bulbs, peeled and finely pounded
3 tbsp. fish sauce
1/4 cup lime juice

Mix all the ingredients together.

PREPARATION

1. Remove the skin and the inedible portions of the squid, wash well, carve the flesh in a crosshatch pattern, and then cut into bite-sized pieces.

2. Immerse the squid in boiling water for a short time, then remove and drain.

3. Place the squid in a bowl, add the onion, ginger, celery, and mint leaves, pour on the dressing and toss gently.

4. Transfer to a plate with lettuce, garnish with the spur chilli, carrot and serve.

เครื่องปรุง

ปลาหมึกกล้วย 500 กรัม
ขิงอ่อนซอย 1/2 ถ้วย
หอมใหญ่หั่นแว่นบาง ๆ 1 หัว
ขึ้นฉ่ายหั่นท่อนสั้น 1 ถ้วย
สะระแหน่เด็ดเป็นใบ 1/4 ถ้วย
พริกชี้ฟ้าแดงหั่นฝอย 1 เม็ด

เครื่องปรุงน้ำยำ

พริกขี้หนูสวนโขลกละเอียด 10 เม็ด
กระเทียมปอกเปลือกโขลกละเอียด 3 หัว
น้ำปลา 3 ช้อนโต๊ะ
น้ำมะนาว 1/4 ถ้วย
ผสมเครื่องปรุงทั้งหมดเข้าด้วยกัน

วิธีทำ

1. ลอกเยื่อปลาหมึกออก เอาส่วนที่รับประทานไม่ได้ออก ล้างให้สะอาด บั้งเป็นตาตาราง หั่นชิ้นพอคำ

2. ต้มน้ำให้เดือด ใส่ปลาหมึกลงลวกเร็ว ๆ ตักขึ้นให้สะเด็ดน้ำ

3. ใส่ปลาหมึกลงในชามผสม ใส่หอมใหญ่ ขิง ขึ้น-ฉ่าย สะระแหน่ ราดด้วยน้ำยำ เคล้าเบา ๆ

4. ตักใส่จานที่ตกแต่งด้วยผักกาดหอม แครอท โรยพริกชี้ฟ้าแดงหั่นฝอย เสิร์ฟ

KUNG KAMKRAM PHLA
Charcoal-broiled prawns with spice dressing
กุ้งก้ามกรามพล่า

INGREDIENTS

2 large spiny-clawed prawns
2 tbsp. finely sliced lemon grass
2 sliced hot chillies
1 tbsp. thinly sliced shallot
1 tsp. finely sliced kaffir lime leaf
1 tsp. chopped garlic
2 tsp. fish sauce
2 tbsp. lime juice
1 tbsp. roasted chilli paste
1/4 cup mint leaves

PREPARATION

1. Wash the prawns, cut off the feelers, split open along the back from head to tail, and remove the veins.

2. Broil slowly over coals of a low charcoal fire, turning frequently. When just done (beware of overcooking) remove to a serving dish.

3. Mix the chilli paste into the fish sauce and lime juice. The taste should be sour, salty and slightly sweet.

4. Mix the lemon grass, chillies, shallot, garlic, and kaffir lime leaf into the sauce and then pour over the prawns. Sprinkle with mint. Serve.

เครื่องปรุง

กุ้งก้ามกรามตัวใหญ่ 2 ตัว
ตะไคร้ซอย 2 ช้อนโต๊ะ
พริกขี้หนูซอย 2 เม็ด
หอมแดงซอย 1 ช้อนโต๊ะ
ใบมะกรูดหั่นฝอย 1 ช้อนชา
กระเทียมสับ 1 ช้อนชา
น้ำปลา 2 ช้อนชา
น้ำมะนาว 2 ช้อนโต๊ะ
น้ำพริกเผา 1 ช้อนโต๊ะ
สะระแหน่เด็ดเป็นใบ 1/4 ถ้วย

วิธีทำ

1. ล้างกุ้งให้สะอาด สับหนวดทิ้ง ผ่าหลังทั้งเปลือก ชักเส้นดำออก

2. นำกุ้งไปย่างบนเตาถ่าน ไฟอ่อน พลิกไปมาพอสุก (อย่าให้สุกมาก) วางไว้บนจาน

3. ผสมน้ำพริกเผา น้ำปลา น้ำมะนาวเข้าด้วยกัน ชิมดูให้มีรสเปรี้ยว เค็ม หวานเล็กน้อย เป็นน้ำปรุง

4. ผสมตะไคร้ พริกขี้หนู หอมแดง กระเทียม ใบ-มะกรูด ลงเคล้ากับน้ำปรุงที่เตรียมไว้ แล้วนำไปราดบนตัวกุ้ง โรยใบสะระแหน่ เสิร์ฟ

YAM SAM SAO
Cockles, mussels, and clams in spicy salad
ยำสามสาว

INGREDIENTS

10 cockles, 15 mussels, 20 clams,
2 tbsp. thinly sliced shallot
2 tbsp. thinly sliced lemon grass
1 tbsp. crushed hot chilli
1 tbsp. roasted chilli paste
1/4 cup mint leaves
1 1/2 tbsp. fish sauce
2 tbsp. lime juice, 1/2 tsp. sugar
3 lettuce leaves

PREPARATION

1. Place the cockles, mussels, and clams in fresh water and let them be for a long enough time that they open their shells and expel any sand or mud inside them. Then wash well in plenty of water several times until really clean, and then put in a colander to drain.

2. Lower the colander into a pot and pour in enough boiling water to cover the shells. After a few minutes, remove from the water, allow to cool, open, reserve the insides, and discard the shells.

3. Mix the fish sauce, lime juice, sugar, chilli, and chilli paste together well, taste to see if the balance of the hot, sour, and salty tastes is right; if not, season accordingly. Then, pour in the cockles, mussels, and clams, stir quickly to mix, and add the shallot and lemon grass.

4. Spoon onto a bed of lettuce leaves on a serving plate, sprinkle with the mint, and serve immediately.

เครื่องปรุง

หอยแครง 10 ตัว
หอยแมลงภู่ 15 ตัว
หอยลาย 20 ตัว
หอมแดงซอย 2 ช้อนโต๊ะ
ตะไคร้ซอย 2 ช้อนโต๊ะ
พริกขี้หนูบุบ 1 ช้อนโต๊ะ
น้ำพริกเผา 1 ช้อนโต๊ะ
สะระแหน่เด็ดเป็นใบ 1/4 ถ้วย
น้ำปลา 1 1/2 ช้อนโต๊ะ
น้ำมะนาว 2 ช้อนโต๊ะ
น้ำตาลทราย 1/2 ช้อนชา
ผักกาดหอม 3 ใบ

วิธีทำ

1. ล้างหอยแครง หอยแมลงภู่ หอยลาย ให้สะอาด โดยแช่น้ำทิ้งไว้นานๆ เพื่อให้หอยอ้าปากคายดินออกมา แล้วจึงล้างผ่านน้ำหลายๆครั้งจนแน่ใจว่าสะอาดแล้ว ใส่ตะแกรงพักไว้ให้สะเด็ดน้ำ

2. ต้มน้ำให้เดือด นำน้ำต้มเดือดไปเทลวกหอยที่อยู่ในตะแกรงให้หอยพอสุกประมาณ 2-3 นาที แกะเอาแต่เนื้อใส่จานไว้

3. ผสมน้ำยำ ด้วยการนำเอาน้ำปลาผสมกับน้ำ-มะนาว น้ำตาล พริกขี้หนู น้ำพริกเผา เคล้ากันให้ทั่ว ชิมรสเพื่อปรับแต่งตามใจชอบอีกครั้ง ให้มีเผ็ด เปรี้ยว เค็ม แล้วจึงเอาหอยที่ลวกไว้แล้ว ลงคลุกกับน้ำยำให้ทั่วอย่างเร็วๆ ใส่หอมแดง ตะไคร้

4. จัดใส่จานที่มีผักกาดหอมรองอยู่ โรยหน้าด้วยสะระแหน่ จัดเสิร์ฟทันที

YAM HOI SHELL
Spicy scallop salad
ยำหอยเชลล์

INGREDIENTS

300	grams scallops
1	onion
10	hot chillies
1	large tomato
1	lettuce plant
2	Chinese celery plants, cut into short lengths
1	cucumber, sliced
2-3	tbsp. lime juice
1	tbsp. fish sauce

PREPARATION

1. Remove the scallops from the shells, wash, dip in boiling water until cooked, and drain.

2. Slice the onion and tomato. Just break open the chillies in a mortar.

3. Toss the scallops, chillies, onion, celery, and tomato together, adding fish sauce and lime juice to taste.

4. Wash the lettuce and lay the leaves on a serving plate; then, put the scallops onto the bed of greens with sliced cucumber.

เครื่องปรุง

หอยเชลล์ 300 กรัม
หอมใหญ่ 1 หัว
พริกขี้หนู 10 เม็ด
มะเขือเทศ 1 ลูก
ผักกาดหอม 1 ต้น
แตงกวาหั่น 1 ลูก
ขึ้นฉ่ายหั่นท่อนสั้น 2 ต้น
น้ำมะนาว 2-3 ช้อนโต๊ะ
น้ำปลา 1 ช้อนโต๊ะ

วิธีทำ

1. แกะหอยเชลล์เอาแต่เนื้อ ล้างให้สะอาด นำไปลวกในน้ำเดือดจนสุก ตักขึ้นให้สะเด็ดน้ำ

2. หั่นหอมใหญ่ตามขวาง หั่นมะเขือเทศเป็นชิ้น บุบพริกขี้หนูทั้งเม็ด

3. เคล้าหอยเชลล์กับหอมใหญ่ พริกขี้หนู ขึ้นฉ่าย มะเขือเทศ ปรุงรสด้วยน้ำปลา น้ำมะนาว ชิมรสตามชอบ

4. ล้างผักกาดหอม แตงกวา วางรองจาน ตักยำหอยเชลล์วางบนจาน

KHAW MU YANG KHA-NA KROB
Broiled pork jowl and crisp kale
คอหมูย่างคะน้ากรอบ

INGREDIENTS
500 grams pork jowl, 500 grams
Chinese kale, 1 garlic bulb, 1 tsp. finely
sliced coriander root, 1 tsp. ground pepper,
2 tsp. sugar, 2 tbsp. seasoning sauce

SPICY SAUCE
Mix together : 2 tsp. finely sliced hot chilli
3 tbsp. finely sliced garlic, 1 tsp. sugar
3 tbsp. fish sauce, 3 tbsp. lime juice

PREPARATION
1. Wash the pork well, and cut into 1/2 inch thick slices.

2. Pound the garlic, coriander root, and pepper until well mashed. Rub this into the pork. Next, add the sugar and seasoning sauce and work the pork around in these. Then, set aside and allow to marinate for about thirty minutes.

3. Wash the kale well. Remove and discard the leafy portions; only the stems will be used. Peel the stems, cut them into sections about three inches long. Cut each section lengthwise into thin slices, and immediately put them on ice to keep them crisp and drain.

4. Broil the pork over a medium charcoal fire until golden brown, and then cut into thin slices.

5. Arrange the slices of pork and kale on a platter, pour the sauce over them, and serve.

เครื่องปรุง
เนื้อหมูส่วนคอ 500 กรัม
ผักคะน้า 500 กรัม
กระเทียม 1 หัว
รากผักชีหั่นละเอียด 1 ช้อนชา
พริกไทยป่น 1 ช้อนชา
น้ำตาลทราย 2 ช้อนชา
ซอสปรุงรส 2 ช้อนโต๊ะ

เครื่องปรุงน้ำปรุงรส
พริกขี้หนูซอย 2 ช้อนชา
กระเทียมหั่นบาง ๆ 3 ช้อนโต๊ะ
น้ำตาลทราย 1 ช้อนชา
น้ำปลา 3 ช้อนโต๊ะ
น้ำมะนาว 3 ช้อนโต๊ะ
ผสมเครื่องปรุงทั้งหมดเข้าด้วยกัน

วิธีทำ
1. ล้างเนื้อหมูให้สะอาด แล่เป็นชิ้นหนา 1/2 นิ้ว

2. โขลกกระเทียม รากผักชี พริกไทย ให้ละเอียด แล้วเคล้ากับหมู ใส่น้ำตาล ซอสปรุงรส เคล้าให้เข้ากัน หมักไว้ประมาณ 30 นาที

3. ล้างผักคะน้าให้สะอาด ตัดเอาเฉพาะส่วนต้น ปอกเปลือกเอาแต่ส่วนใน หั่นท่อนยาวประมาณ 3 นิ้ว หั่นบาง ๆตามยาว แล้วนำลงแช่ในน้ำแข็งทันที เพื่อให้คะน้ามีความกรอบ สงขึ้นให้สะเด็ดน้ำ

4. ย่างเนื้อหมูบนเตาถ่าน ใช้ไฟกลาง ย่างจนสุกเหลือง แล้วนำมาหั่นเป็นชิ้นบาง ๆ

5. จัดคอหมูย่างพร้อมคะน้ากรอบใส่จาน ราดด้วยน้ำปรุงรส เสิร์ฟ

YAM SAM SAHAI

Three companions spicy salad

ยำสามสหาย

INGREDIENTS

200 grams steamed pork tenderloin, cut diagonally into thin slices

200 grams steamed chicken meat, cut diagonally into thin slices

200 grams steamed shelled white prawn, cut diagonally into thin slices

1/2 cup shredded Chinese radish

1/2 cup shredded carrot

1/4 cup mint leaves

1/4 cup short sections of Chinese celery

DRESSING INGREDIENTS

2 dried large chillies, roasted and then pounded well

2 garlic bulbs, roasted and then pounded well

1 tbsp. sugar, 2 tbsp. fish sauce

1/4 cup lime juice, 3 tbsp. tamarind juice

Mix the dried chillies, garlic, sugar, fish sauce, and tamarind juice in a pot, and heat. When the mixture boils, remove from the heat, and set aside. When cool, add the lime juice and stir to mix.

PREPARATION

1. Toss the pork, chicken, and prawn with the dressing. Add the celery, toss to mix, and then add the mint leaves.

2. Transfer to a plate, and arrange the Chinese radish and carrot alongside.

เครื่องปรุง

เนื้อหมูสันนอกนึ่งหั่นแฉลบบาง ๆ 200 กรัม

ไก่นึ่งหั่นแฉลบบาง ๆ 200 กรัม

กุ้งชีแฮ้นึ่งแกะเปลือกหั่นแฉลบ 200 กรัม

หัวไชเท้าใส 1/2 ถ้วย

แครอทใส 1/2 ถ้วย

สะระแหน่เด็ดเป็นใบ 1/4 ถ้วย

ขึ้นฉ่ายหั่นท่อนสั้น 1/4 ถ้วย

เครื่องปรุงน้ำยำ

พริกแห้งเผาโขลกละเอียด 2 เม็ด

กระเทียมเผาโขลกละเอียด 2 หัว

น้ำตาลทราย 1 ช้อนโต๊ะ

น้ำปลา 2 ช้อนโต๊ะ

น้ำมะนาว 1/4 ถ้วย

น้ำมะขามเปียก 3 ช้อนโต๊ะ

ผสมพริกแห้ง กระเทียม น้ำตาล น้ำปลา น้ำ-มะขามเปียก เข้าด้วยกัน ใส่หม้อ ตั้งไฟพอเดือด ยกลง ปล่อยให้เย็น ใส่น้ำมะนาว คนให้ทั่ว

วิธีทำ

1. เคล้าเนื้อหมู ไก่ กุ้ง กับน้ำยำ เข้าด้วยกัน ใส่ขึ้นฉ่าย เคล้าพอทั่ว ใส่สะระแหน่

2. ตักใส่จาน จัดเสิร์ฟกับหัวไชเท้าใส แครอทใส

YAM THAI NOI
Spicy pork and prawn salad
ยำไทยน้อย

INGREDIENTS

100 grams small thin slices of boiled pork
2 hard-boiled eggs, cut into thin slices
5 cucumbers, 1 tbsp. coriander leaves
1 onion, cut into thin slices
1 thinly sliced red spur chilli

DRESSING INGREDIENTS

2 red spur chillies
2 garlic bulbs, 7 pepper corns
1/2 tbsp. finely sliced coriander root
1/4 cup sugar, 1/4 cup fish sauce
2 tbsp. lime juice
1/4 cup tamarind juice

Pound the spur chilli, garlic, coriander root, and pepper corns until finely ground, add the sugar, fish sauce, and tamarind juice. When the mixture boils, remove from the heat and set aside. When the mixture is cool, add the lime juice and stir to mix.

PREPARATION

1. Wash and peel the cucumbers, cut decorative grooves down the length of each, and cut across into thick slices.
2. Mix the pork, cucumber, onion, and coriander leaves together in a bowl, add the dressing, and toss gently.
3. Transfer to a plate, garnish with the egg slices, red spur chilli. Serve.

เครื่องปรุง

เนื้อหมูต้มหั่นชิ้นบางเล็ก 100 กรัม
ไข่ต้มสุกแข็งหั่น 2 ฟอง
แตงกวา 5 ลูก
ผักชีเด็ดเป็นใบ 1 ช้อนโต๊ะ
หอมใหญ่หั่นบาง 1 หัว
พริกชี้ฟ้าแดงหั่นฝอย 1 เม็ด

เครื่องปรุงน้ำยำ

พริกชี้ฟ้าแดง 2 เม็ด
กระเทียม 2 หัว
พริกไทยเม็ด 7 เม็ด
รากผักชีหั่นละเอียด 1/2 ช้อนโต๊ะ
น้ำตาลทราย 1/4 ถ้วย
น้ำปลา 1/4 ถ้วย
น้ำมะนาว 2 ช้อนโต๊ะ
น้ำมะขามเปียก 1/4 ถ้วย

โขลกพริกชี้ฟ้า กระเทียม รากผักชี พริกไทย รวมกันให้ละเอียด ผสมกับน้ำตาล น้ำปลา น้ำมะขาม-เปียก ใส่หม้อตั้งไฟ พอเดือด ยกลง ปล่อยให้เย็น ใส่น้ำมะนาว คนให้ทั่ว

วิธีทำ

1. ล้างแตงกวาให้สะอาด ปอกเปลือก จักหยาบ ๆ รอบลูก หั่นตามขวางหนา ๆ
2. เคล้าหมู แตงกวา หอมใหญ่ ผักชี ในชามผสม ราดด้วยน้ำยำ เคล้าเบา ๆ
3. จัดใส่จาน แต่งด้วยไข่ต้ม พริกชี้ฟ้าแดง เสิร์ฟ

YAM KHAMOI
Thieves' spicy salad
ยำขโมย

INGREDIENTS

100 grams thin slices of boiled pork
100 grams thin slices of boiled prawn
1 hard-boiled egg, 1 lettuce plant
2 cucumbers, sliced
1 onion, cut into thin slices
1 tbsp. coriander leaves
1/4 cup mint leaves
1 thinly sliced red spur chilli

DRESSING INGREDIENTS

2 red spur chillies, 1 garlic bulb
1/2 tbsp. pounded coriander root
3 pepper corns, 2 tbsp. sugar
2 tbsp. fish sauce
2 tbsp. lime juice, 3 tbsp. vinegar

Pound the chillies, garlic, coriander root, and pepper corns until well ground, add the sugar, fish sauce, vinegar, and lime juice, and stir to mix. Taste and adjust as required.

PREPARATION

1. Wash the lettuce and cut into short pieces. Wash and peel the cucumber and slice diagonally.
2. Place the pork, prawn, lettuce, cucumber, onion, and coriander and mint leaves together in a bowl, add the dressing, and toss gently.
3. Transfer to a plate, garnish with slices of egg and spur chilli, and serve.

เครื่องปรุง

เนื้อหมูต้มหั่นชิ้นบาง 100 กรัม
กุ้งต้มหั่นชิ้นบาง 100 กรัม
ไข่ต้มสุกแข็ง 1 ฟอง
ผักกาดหอม 1 ต้น
แตงกวาหั่น 2 ลูก
หอมใหญ่หั่นแว่นบาง 1 หัว
ผักชีเด็ดเป็นใบ 1 ช้อนโต๊ะ
สะระแหน่เด็ดเป็นใบ 1/4 ถ้วย
พริกชี้ฟ้าแดงหั่นฝอย 1 เม็ด

เครื่องปรุงน้ำยำ

พริกชี้ฟ้าแดง 2 เม็ด
กระเทียม 1 หัว
รากผักชีโขลก 1/2 ช้อนโต๊ะ
พริกไทยเม็ด 3 เม็ด
น้ำตาลทราย 2 ช้อนโต๊ะ
น้ำปลา 2 ช้อนโต๊ะ
น้ำมะนาว 2 ช้อนโต๊ะ
น้ำส้มสายชู 3 ช้อนโต๊ะ
โขลกพริกชี้ฟ้า กระเทียม รากผักชี พริกไทย ให้ละเอียด ผสมกับน้ำตาล น้ำปลา น้ำส้มสายชู น้ำมะนาว คนให้เข้ากัน ชิมรส

วิธีทำ

1. ล้างผักกาดหอมให้สะอาด หั่นท่อนสั้น ล้างแตงกวา ปอกเปลือก หั่นแฉลบเอาแต่เนื้อ
2. ผสมเนื้อหมู กุ้ง ผักกาดหอม แตงกวา หอมใหญ่ ผักชี สะระแหน่ ราดด้วยน้ำยำ เคล้าเบาๆ
3. ตักใส่จาน แต่งด้วยไข่ต้ม โรยพริกชี้ฟ้าแดงหั่นฝอย เสิร์ฟ

YAM KAI YANG
Barbecued chicken spicy salad
ยำไก่ย่าง

INGREDIENTS

1   **barbecued chicken**
2   **spring shallots, cut into thin slices**
2   **bell chillies, cut into thin slices and blanched**
1 1/2   **tbsp. finely sliced garlic**
1   **thinly sliced red spur chilli**
1/2   **cup mint leaves**
2   **tbsp. finely sliced kaffir lime leaves**
1/2   **cup shredded green mango**
1/2   **cup pan-roasted peanuts**

DRESSING INGREDIENTS

1/2   **tbsp. roasted dried large chilli, pounded**
1/2   **tbsp. sugar**
3   **tbsp. fish sauce**
3   **tbsp. lime juice**

Mix all the ingredients in a pot, and heat. When the mixture comes to a boil, remove from the heat.

PREPARATION

1. Cut the chicken into thin slices.
2. Toss the chicken and the dressing together. Add the chilli, spring shallots, garlic, mint and kaffir lime leaves, mango, and peanuts, and toss gently.
3. Transfer to a plate, sprinkle with the spur chilli. Serve.

เครื่องปรุง

ไก่ย่าง 1 ตัว
ต้นหอมซอย 2 ต้น
พริกหยวกหั่นบาง ฯลวก 2 เม็ด
กระเทียมซอย 1 1/2 ช้อนโต๊ะ
พริกชี้ฟ้าแดงหั่นฝอย 1 เม็ด
สะระแหน่เด็ดเป็นใบ 1/2 ถ้วย
ใบมะกรูดหั่นฝอย 2 ช้อนโต๊ะ
มะม่วงสับ 1/2 ถ้วย
ถั่วลิสงคั่ว 1/2 ถ้วย

เครื่องปรุงน้ำยำ

พริกแห้งคั่วโขลกละเอียด 1/2 ช้อนโต๊ะ
น้ำตาลทราย 1/2 ช้อนโต๊ะ
น้ำปลา 3 ช้อนโต๊ะ
น้ำมะนาว 3 ช้อนโต๊ะ
ผสมเครื่องปรุงทั้งหมดเข้าด้วยกัน ตั้งไฟพอเดือด ยกลง

วิธีทำ

1. หั่นไก่ย่างเป็นชิ้นบาง ๆ
2. เคล้าไก่ย่างกับน้ำยำเข้าด้วยกัน ใส่พริกหยวก ต้นหอม กระเทียม สะระแหน่ ใบมะกรูด มะม่วงสับ และถั่วลิสงคั่ว เคล้าเบา ๆ
3. ตักใส่จาน โรยด้วยพริกชี้ฟ้าแดง เสิร์ฟ

YAM THALE ROD DED
Prawns, mussels, crab and squid in spicy salad
ยำทะเลรสเด็ด

INGREDIENTS
200	grams	white prawns
100	grams	shelled mussels
100	grams	squid
4	steamed	crab sculls
10	hot	chillies
5	cloves	garlic
3	tbsp.	lime juice
2	tbsp.	fish sauce
1/2	tsp.	sugar
1/2	cup	Chinese celery, cut short
		lettuce, onion

เครื่องปรุง
กุ้งแชบ๊วย 200 กรัม
หอยแมลงภู่ลวกแกะเปลือกออก 100 กรัม
ปลาหมึก 100 กรัม
กรรเชียงปู 4 ชิ้น
พริกขี้หนู 10 เม็ด
กระเทียม 5 กลีบ
น้ำมะนาว 3 ช้อนโต๊ะ
น้ำปลา 2 ช้อนโต๊ะ
น้ำตาลทราย 1/2 ช้อนชา
ขึ้นฉ่ายหั่นท่อน 1/2 ถ้วย
ผักกาดหอม, หอมใหญ่

PREPARATION
1. Wash the lettuce, onion, then slice and arrange on a serving dish.
2. Shell, vein and wash the prawns, reserving the meat only. Clean and wash the squid, cut into bite-sized pieces, and score them attractively. Immerse in boiling water, the prawn, the squid, and the mussels, each seperately and for one minute.
3. Arrange the shell-fish on the serving dish.
4. Pound the chillies and garlic well in a mortar, mix with the lime juice, fish sauce, and sugar, pour over the shell-fish and celery, toss gently, then arrange on the dish and serve.

วิธีทำ
1. ล้างผักกาดหอม หอมใหญ่ หั่นแล้วจัดวางบนจานให้สวยงาม
2. แกะเปลือกกุ้ง หอยแมลงภู่ เอาแต่เนื้อ ล้างปลาหมึก หั่นชิ้นขนาดพอคำ บั้งให้สวยงาม ลวกแต่ละอย่าง ในน้ำเดือด 1 นาที ตักขึ้นให้สะเด็ดน้ำ นึ่งกรรเชียงปูพอสุก
3. จัดอาหารทะเล กุ้ง หอย ปลาหมึก กรรเชียงปู ลงบนจานผักที่จัดไว้
4. โขลกพริกขี้หนู กระเทียม ให้ละเอียด ผสมน้ำมะนาว น้ำปลา น้ำตาล คนให้เข้ากัน ราดส่วนผสมลงบนจานกุ้ง หอย ปลาหมึก กรรเชียงปู และขึ้นฉ่าย คนพอเข้ากัน จัดใส่จาน เสิร์ฟ

YAM HOI KHRAENG

Spicy cockle salad

ยำหอยแครง

INGREDIENTS

800-1,000 grams cockles

1 lettuce plant

1 tbsp. thinly sliced shallot

1 tsp. thinly sliced hot chilli

1 tbsp. thinly sliced young ginger

1 tbsp. finely sliced lemon grass

1/4 cup mint leaves

1 tsp. thinly sliced kaffir lime leaves

2 tbsp. lime juice

1 1/2 tbsp. fish sauce

PREPARATION

1. Soak the cockles in water until they open up and expel any dirt inside. Wash well, cover with boiling water for a few minutes, and shell.

2. Mix the cockles with the lemon grass, shallot, chilli, fish sauce, and lime juice, varying proportions to taste.

3. Spoon the cockles onto the lettuce, sprinkle with mint leaves, kaffir lime leaves and serve.

เครื่องปรุง

หอยแครง 800-1,000 กรัม

ผักกาดหอมเด็ดเป็นใบ 1 ต้น

หอมแดงซอย 1 ช้อนโต๊ะ

พริกขี้หนูซอย 1 ช้อนชา

ขิงอ่อนซอย 1 ช้อนโต๊ะ

ใบมะกรูดซอย 1 ช้อนชา

สะระแหน่เด็ดเป็นใบ 1/4 ถ้วย

ตะไคร้ซอย 1 ช้อนโต๊ะ

น้ำมะนาว 2 ช้อนโต๊ะ

น้ำปลา 1 1/2 ช้อนโต๊ะ

วิธีทำ

1. แช่หอยในน้ำจนปากหอยเปิดและคายสิ่งสกปรก ออก ล้างหอยแครง แล้วลวกให้สุกในน้ำเดือด 2-3 นาที แกะเอาแต่เนื้อ

2. นำหอยแครงมาเคล้ากับตะไคร้ หอมแดง ขิงอ่อน พริกขี้หนู น้ำปลา น้ำมะนาว ให้เข้ากันทั่ว ชิมรส

3. ตักใส่จานที่รองด้วยด้วยผักกาดหอม ตักยำหอย- แครงใส่ในจาน โรยด้วยใบสะระแหน่ ใบมะกรูด

YAM MAENG KAPHRUN

Spicy jellyfish salad

ยำแมงกะพรุน

INGREDIENTS

2 cups jellyfish, cleaned and cut bite-sized

1/2   thinly sliced onion

2   thinly sliced shallots

8-10   crushed hot chillies

1   tsp. thinly sliced red spur chillies

1 1/2   tbsp. fish sauce

2   tbsp. lime juice

เครื่องปรุง

แมงกะพรุนล้างหั่นชิ้นพอคำ 2 ถ้วย

หอมใหญ่หั่นตามขวาง 1/2 หัว

หอมแดงซอย 2 หัว

พริกขี้หนูบุบ 8-10 เม็ด

พริกชี้ฟ้าแดงหั่นฝอย 1 ช้อนชา

น้ำปลา 1 1/2 ช้อนโต๊ะ

น้ำมะนาว 2 ช้อนโต๊ะ

PREPARATION

1. Immerse the jellyfish in boiling water then remove and immediately plunge into cold water for a few moment. After removing from the water, drain. This will give the jellyfish the right munchy texture.

2. Toss the jellyfish with the onion, shallot, and chillies, seasoning to taste with fish sauce and lime juice. Put onto a plate on which lettuce has been arranged and decorate with slices of red spur chilli.

วิธีทำ

1. ลวกแมงกะพรุนในน้ำเดือด แล้วจึงแช่ในน้ำเย็นทันที สักครู่ก็เอาขึ้นให้สะเด็ดน้ำ เพื่อให้เนื้อแมง-กะพรุนกรอบ

2. เคล้าแมงกะพรุนกับหอมใหญ่ หอมแดง พริก-ขี้หนู ปรุงรสด้วยน้ำปลา น้ำมะนาว ชิมรส ตักใส่จานที่แต่งด้วยผักกาดหอม และโรยพริกชี้ฟ้าแดง

YAM PLA FU

Crispy shredded catfish spicy salad

ยำปลาฟู

INGREDIENTS

2 broiled catfishes, 1 lettuce plant
1 thinly sliced red spur chilli, 2 tbsp. fried
peanuts, oil for deep frying

DRESSING INGREDIENTS

5 hot chillies, pounded to break them open
1/4 cup shredded green mango
2 tbsp. thinly sliced shallot
2 tbsp. palm sugar, 3 tbsp. fish sauce
Mix the chillies, sugar, and fish sauce together, add the mango and shallot, and toss to mix thoroughly. Season obtain to a sweet, salty or sour flavor.

PREPARATION

1. Separate the flesh of the catfish from the skin and bones. Break the flesh into shreds with a fork, and then set aside to dry.
2. Place the oil in a wok on medium heat. When the oil is hot, put about half a cup of the catfish in the oil and spread it out into shreds. When the fish starts to brown, gather the shreds together, turn over, and fry until crisp and golden brown. Then, remove from the wok and set aside to drain and cool. Fry the rest of the fish in the same way, half a cup at a time.
3. Toss the cooled catfish with the dressing and the peanuts.
4. Place the catfish on a bed of lettuce arranged on a plate, garnish with chilli slices, and serve.

เครื่องปรุง

ปลาดุกย่าง 2 ตัว
ผักกาดหอมเด็ดเป็นใบ 1 ต้น
พริกชี้ฟ้าแดงหั่นฝอย 1 เม็ด
ถั่วลิสงทอด 2 ช้อนโต๊ะ
น้ำมันสำหรับทอด

เครื่องปรุงน้ำยำ

พริกขี้หนูบุบพอแตก 5 เม็ด
มะม่วงสับ 1/4 ถ้วย
หอมแดงซอย 2 ช้อนโต๊ะ
น้ำตาลปีบ 2 ช้อนโต๊ะ
น้ำปลา 3 ช้อนโต๊ะ
ผสมพริกขี้หนู น้ำตาล น้ำปลา เข้าด้วยกัน ใส่มะม่วง หอมแดง เคล้าให้เข้ากัน ชิมให้ได้ 3 รส

วิธีทำ

1. แกะเนื้อปลา ยีให้ละเอียด ผึ่งให้แห้ง
2. ใส่น้ำมันลงในกระทะ ตั้งไฟให้ร้อน ใช้ไฟกลาง ใส่เนื้อปลาลงทอดครั้งละประมาณ 1/2 ถ้วย โปรยให้เนื้อปลากระจาย ทอดสักครู่พอเริ่มเหลืองเขี่ยเนื้อปลารวมกัน แล้วกลับอีกด้านหนึ่ง ให้เหลืองทั้งสองด้าน ตักขึ้น พักไว้ให้สะเด็ดน้ำมัน และทิ้งให้เนื้อปลาที่ทอดเย็นลง
3. เคล้าเนื้อปลาฟู น้ำยำ ถั่วลิสง เบาๆ ให้เข้ากัน
4. ตักใส่จานที่รองด้วยผักกาดหอม โรยด้วยพริกชี้-ฟ้าแดงหั่นฝอย เสิร์ฟ

YAM PLA SALIT FU
Spicy shredded gourami salad
ยำปลาสลิดฟู

INGREDIENTS

3-4	gouramies about 300 grams
3	Chinese celery hearts
3 tbsp.	shredded sour green mango
1 tbsp.	finely sliced hot chilli
2 tbsp.	fried cashew nuts
3 tbsp.	finely sliced shallot
1 tbsp.	palm sugar
3 tbsp.	fish sauce
4 tbsp.	lime juice
	oil for frying

PREPARATION

1. Fillet the gouramies. Cut each fillet in half. With a fork, break up the flesh into fluffy shreds. Fry the shredded fish in plenty of oil until crisp, and then drain.

2. Put the sugar, fish sauce, and lime juice in a pot, bring to a boil over low heat, and then remove from heat and allow to cool.

3. Place the fried fish on a plate, sprinkle it with the shallot, mango, and cashews and garnish with the celery heart. Just before serving, mix the chilli into the sauce from Step 2 and pour over the salad.

เครื่องปรุง

ปลาสลิด น้ำหนัก 300 กรัม 3-4 ตัว
ขึ้นฉ่ายยอดอ่อนๆ 3 ช่อ
มะม่วงดิบสับ (เปรี้ยว) 3 ช้อนโต๊ะ
พริกขี้หนูซอย 1 ช้อนโต๊ะ
เม็ดมะม่วงหิมพานต์ทอด 2 ช้อนโต๊ะ
หอมแดงซอย 3 ช้อนโต๊ะ
น้ำตาลปีบ 1 ช้อนโต๊ะ
น้ำปลา 3 ช้อนโต๊ะ
น้ำมะนาว 4 ช้อนโต๊ะ
น้ำมันสำหรับทอด

วิธีทำ

1. แล่ปลาสลิดเอาก้างกลางออกแบ่งเป็น 2 ชิ้น ใช้ส้อมเกลี่ยเนื้อให้ปุยๆ แล้วนำไปทอดให้กรอบในน้ำมันมาก พักไว้

2. ใส่น้ำตาล น้ำปลา น้ำมะนาว ลงในหม้อ เคี่ยวไฟอ่อน พอเดือด ยกลง ทิ้งไว้ให้เย็น

3. จัดปลาสลิดที่ทอดลงในจาน โรยหอมแดง มะม่วง เม็ดมะม่วงหิมพานต์ แต่งด้วยยอดขึ้นฉ่าย แยกน้ำยำที่เคี่ยว (ส่วนผสมข้อ 2) ใส่พริกขี้หนู ราดน้ำยำขณะที่เสิร์ฟ

YAM SOM-O
Pomelo spicy salad
ยำส้มโอ

INGREDIENTS

2 cups pomelo flesh
1/2 cup thin slices of shelled steamed prawn
1/4 cup pan-roasted shredded coconut meat
1/4 cup coarsely ground pan-roasted peanut
1 tbsp. sauted shallot slices
1 thinly sliced red spur chilli
1 tsp. thinly sliced kaffir lime leaves
1 tbsp. coriander leaves

DRESSING INGREDIENTS

1 dried large chilli, roasted until fragrant
1 tbsp. well-pounded dried knife fish
2 roasted shallots, 1 roasted garlic bulb
3 tbsp. palm sugar, 3 tbsp. fish sauce
3 tbsp. tamarind juice

Pound the chilli, fish, shallots and garlic until well ground. Transfer to a pot, add the fish sauce, sugar, and tamarind juice, and simmer until thickened.

PREPARATION

1. Place the pomelo in a bowl, add the prawn, and then pour on the dressing. Add the coconut, the peanuts, and half a tablespoonful of the sauted shallot, and toss gently until thoroughly mixed.
2. Transfer the salad onto a plate, sprinkle with the remaining sauted shallot, spur chilli, kaffir lime leaves and the coriander leaves. Serve.

เครื่องปรุง

ส้มโอแกะเอาแต่เนื้อ 2 ถ้วย
กุ้งนึ่งแกะเปลือกหั่นบาง ๆ 1/2 ถ้วย
มะพร้าวขูดคั่ว 1/4 ถ้วย
ถั่วลิสงคั่วโขลกหยาบ ๆ 1/4 ถ้วย
หอมแดงเจียว 1 ช้อนโต๊ะ
พริกชี้ฟ้าแดงหั่นฝอย 1 เม็ด
ใบมะกรูดหั่นฝอย 1 ช้อนชา
ผักชีเด็ดเป็นใบ 1 ช้อนโต๊ะ

เครื่องปรุงน้ำยำ

พริกแห้งคั่วให้หอม 1 เม็ด
ปลากรอบย่างโขลกละเอียด 1 ช้อนโต๊ะ
หอมแดงเผา 2 หัว
กระเทียมเผา 1 หัว
น้ำตาลปีบ 3 ช้อนโต๊ะ
น้ำปลา 3 ช้อนโต๊ะ
น้ำมะขามเปียก 3 ช้อนโต๊ะ
โขลกพริกแห้ง ปลากรอบ หอมแดง กระเทียม เข้า ด้วยกันให้ละเอียด แล้วผสมกับน้ำปลา น้ำตาล น้ำมะขามเปียก ตั้งไฟกลาง เคี่ยวพอข้น ยกลง

วิธีทำ

1. ใส่ส้มโอในชามผสม ใส่กุ้ง ราดด้วยน้ำยำ ใส่ มะพร้าวคั่ว ถั่วลิสงคั่ว หอมแดงเจียว 1/2 ช้อนโต๊ะ เคล้าเบา ๆ พอทั่ว
2. ตักใส่ภาชนะ โรยหอมแดงเจียว พริกชี้ฟ้าแดง หั่นฝอย ใบมะกรูด ผักชี เสิร์ฟ

YAM CHOM-PHU
Rose apple spicy salad
ยำชมพู่

INGREDIENTS

6   rose apples or any kind of apple, sliced

100   grams thin slice of steamed prawn meat

DRESSING INGREDIENTS

1   tbsp. roasted chilli paste, medium hot

2   tbsp. lime juice

1   tbsp. ground dried shrimp

2   tbsp. water

PREPARATION

1. Mix all the ingredient together.

2. Place the rose apples and prawn in a bowl. Pour on the dressing and toss gently.

3. Transfer to a plate and serve.

เครื่องปรุง

ชมพู่เขียวผ่าครึ่งหั่นบาง ๆ 6   ลูก

กุ้งนึ่งแกะเปลือกหั่นบาง ๆ 100   กรัม

เครื่องปรุงน้ำยำ

น้ำพริกเผา (ชนิดไม่เผ็ด) 1   ช้อนโต๊ะ

น้ำมะนาว 2   ช้อนโต๊ะ

ซีอิ๊วขาว 1   ช้อนโต๊ะ

กุ้งแห้งป่น 1   ช้อนโต๊ะ

น้ำ 2   ช้อนโต๊ะ

วิธีทำ

1. ผสมเครื่องน้ำยำเข้าด้วยกัน

2. นำชมพู่และกุ้งวางลงในชามผสม ราดด้วยน้ำยำ เคล้าเบา ๆ พอเข้ากัน

3. ตักใส่จาน เสิร์ฟ

YAM KHAI DAO BACON
Spicy bacon and eggs
ยำไข่ดาวเบคอน

INGREDIENTS

3 eggs
5 strips bacon
3 lettuce leaves
1 tbsp. finely sliced hot chilli
1/4 cup finely sliced onion
1 tsp. sugar
2 tbsp. fish sauce
2 tbsp. lime juice
oil for frying

PREPARATION

1. Place a wok on medium heat. When it is hot, pour in the oil. Allow the oil to become very hot. Break the eggs into a bowl, but do not beat them. Pour the eggs into the center of the oil, fry them up bubbly and crisp, and then remove and set them aside.

2. Fry the bacon until crisp and set aside.

3. Mix the fish sauce, lime juice, and sugar, stir until the sugar dissolves, and then add the chilli.

4. Cut the fried egg into eights and arrange so the egg assumes its original shape. Sprinkle with the onion. Cut the bacon into one-inch lengths and place these on top. Pour the sauce from Step 3 over the egg, decorate with lettuce leaves, carrot, cucumber, and serve.

เครื่องปรุง

ไข่ไก่ 3 ฟอง
เบคอน 5 ชิ้น
ผักกาดหอม 3 ใบ
พริกขี้หนูซอย 1 ช้อนโต๊ะ
หอมใหญ่ซอย 1/4 ถ้วย
น้ำตาลทราย 1 ช้อนชา
น้ำปลา 2 ช้อนโต๊ะ
น้ำมะนาว 2 ช้อนโต๊ะ
น้ำมันสำหรับทอด

วิธีทำ

1. ตั้งกระทะใช้ไฟกลาง พอกระทะร้อนใส่น้ำมัน ให้น้ำมันร้อนจัด ต่อยไข่ใส่ชามรวมกัน ห้ามคน เทตรงกลางน้ำมัน ตักน้ำมันให้ไข่สุกกรอบฟู ตักขึ้นพักไว้

2. ทอดเบคอนให้กรอบ ตักขึ้น พักไว้

3. ผสมน้ำปลา น้ำมะนาว น้ำตาล คนให้ละลาย ใส่พริกขี้หนู

4. หั่นไข่ดาวทอดกรอบเป็น 8 ชิ้น วางรูปเดิม วางหอมใหญ่ ตัดเบคอนเป็นท่อนยาวขนาด 1 นิ้ว วางบนไข่ดาว ราดน้ำยำที่ปรุงไว้ (ส่วนผสมข้อ 3) แต่งด้วยผักกาดหอม แครอท แตงกวา เสิร์ฟ

YAM SAI KRAWK BACON THOD

Spicy bacon-wrapped sausages

ยำไส้กรอกเบคอนทอด

INGREDIENTS

10	pork cocktail sausages
5	strips bacon
2	tomatoes
1/2	onion, cut into thin slices
1	shreds of red spur chilli
5	red hot chillies
1/4	tsp. sugar
1	tbsp. fish sauce
2 1/2	tbsp. lime juice
10	toothpicks
	oil for frying

เครื่องปรุง

ไส้กรอกหมู (ค็อกเทล) 10 อัน

เบคอน 5 ชิ้น

มะเขือเทศ 2 ลูก

หอมใหญ่หั่นแว่นบาง ๆ 1/2 หัว

พริกชี้ฟ้าแดงหั่นฝอย 1 เม็ด

พริกขี้หนูแดง 5 เม็ด

น้ำตาลทราย 1/4 ช้อนชา

น้ำปลา 1 ช้อนโต๊ะ

น้ำมะนาว 2 1/2 ช้อนโต๊ะ

ไม้จิ้มฟัน 10 อัน

น้ำมันสำหรับทอด

PREPARATION

1. Remove the plastic wrappers from the sausages. Cut the bacon strips in half.

2. Wrap a piece of bacon around each sausage, and secure with a toothpick.

3. Deep fry the bacon-wrapped sausages until golden, remove from the oil, allow to cool, and then remove the toothpicks.

4. Mix the fish sauce, lime juice, and sugar, and stir until the sugar dissolves.

5. Crush the chillies, chop them fine, and add to the dressing mixture from Step 4.

6. Arrange the sausages on a plate, pour the dressing over them, and decorate with slices of red spur chilli, tomato and onion, and serve.

วิธีทำ

1. ลอกพลาสติกออกจากไส้กรอก ตัดเบคอนเป็น 2 ท่อน

2. นำเบคอนห่อไส้กรอกทั้งหมด เสียบด้วยไม้จิ้มฟัน

3. นำไส้กรอกที่ห่อลงทอดให้เหลืองอ่อน ๆ ตักขึ้นพักไว้ เอาไม้จิ้มฟันออก

4. ผสมน้ำปลา น้ำมะนาว น้ำตาล คนให้ละลายเข้ากัน

5. ทุบพริกขี้หนูแล้วสับละเอียด ใส่ในน้ำที่ปรุงรส (ส่วนผสมข้อ 4)

6. จัดไส้กรอกใส่จาน ราดด้วยน้ำปรุงรส แต่งด้วยพริกชี้ฟ้าแดง มะเขือเทศ หอมใหญ่ เสิร์ฟ

YAM HU MU PRUNG ROD
Spicy pork ear salad
ยำหูหมูปรุงรส

INGREDIENTS

2 five-spice stewed pork ears
1 tomato, cut into disk-shaped slices
1/2 cup slices of large cucumber
100 grams tender young lettuce
3 sprigs of mint
1 tbsp. finely sliced hot chilli
1 cup finely sliced onion
1 tsp. sugar
3 tbsp. fish sauce
1 tbsp. lime juice
2 tbsp. vinegar

PREPARATION

1. Steam the pork ears until hot, remove from the steamer, allow to cool, cut into thin slices, and place in a mixing bowl.

2. Mix the fish sauce, vinegar, lime juice, and sugar, stir until the sugar dissolves, and add the chilli. Pour this dressing over the pork ear, and toss gently. Add the onion, and toss gently so as to avoid bruising. Arrange the tomato and large cucumber slices and the lettuce on a plate, arrange the pork ear on top, garnish with the mint, and serve.

Note: Hu mu prung rod is the pork's ear boiled, in five spice powder, star anise, poi-kak, โป๊ยกั๊ก, until the pork's ear.

เครื่องปรุง

หูหมูพะโล้ 2 หู
มะเขือเทศหั่นแว่น 1 ลูก
แตงร้านหั่นแว่น 1/2 ถ้วย
ผักกาดหอมอ่อน 100 กรัม
สะระแหน่เด็ดเป็นช่อ 3 ช่อ
พริกขี้หนูซอย 1 ช้อนโต๊ะ
หอมใหญ่ซอย 1 ถ้วย
น้ำตาลทราย 1 ช้อนชา
น้ำปลา 3 ช้อนโต๊ะ
น้ำมะนาว 1 ช้อนโต๊ะ
น้ำส้มสายชู 2 ช้อนโต๊ะ

วิธีทำ

1. นึ่งหูหมูพะโล้พอให้ร้อน ยกลง ทิ้งให้เย็น นำมาหั่นบางๆ ใส่ชามสำหรับผสม

2. ผสมน้ำปลา น้ำส้มสายชู น้ำมะนาว น้ำตาล คนให้ละลาย ใส่พริกขี้หนู ใส่น้ำปรุงรสเคล้ากับหูหมูพะโล้พอเข้ากัน ใส่หอมใหญ่เคล้าเบาๆ ผักจะได้ไม่ช้ำ จัดมะเขือเทศ แตงร้าน ผักกาดหอม ลงจาน ตักยำใส่จาน แต่งด้วยสะระแหน่ เสิร์ฟ

KUNG TEN
Broiled prawns with spicy sauce
กุ้งเต้น

INGREDIENTS
2-3 large spiny clawed prawns
1 lettuce plant, sliced into strips
2 tbsp. chopped hot chillies
2 tbsp. chopped garlic
1/4 cup mint leaves
2 tbsp. lime juice
1 tbsp. fish sauce

PREPARATION
1. Wash the prawns well, and remove the shells and the dark pouch in the head. Broil the prawns until they are nearly done, split them in half lengthwise and place them on a bed of lettuce arranged on a plate.
2. Mix the garlic, chilli, fish sauce, and lime juice to obtain a spicy-hot, sour, salty sauce, pour this over the prawns, sprinkle with the mint leaves and serve.

เครื่องปรุง
กุ้งนางตัวใหญ่ 2-3 ตัว
ผักกาดหอมหั่นเป็นท่อน 1 ต้น
พริกขี้หนูสับ 2 ช้อนโต๊ะ
กระเทียมสับ 2 ช้อนโต๊ะ
สะระแหน่เด็ดเป็นใบ 1/4 ถ้วย
น้ำมะนาว 2 ช้อนโต๊ะ
น้ำปลา 1 ช้อนโต๊ะ

วิธีทำ
1. ล้างกุ้งให้สะอาด แกะเปลือกออก เอาถุงมูลกุ้งบนหัวออก แล้วจึงนำไปย่างไฟให้พอสุกๆดิบๆ นำกุ้งมาผ่าออกเป็นสองซีก จัดใส่จานที่รองด้วยผักกาดหอม
2. ผสมกระเทียม พริกขี้หนู น้ำปลา น้ำมะนาว ปรุงรสเผ็ด เปรี้ยว เค็ม ให้ได้รสจัดตามความต้องการ แล้วจึงนำไปราดบนตัวกุ้งที่เตรียมไว้ โรยสะระแหน่ เสิร์ฟ

PHLA PLA MEUK
Spicy boiled squid
พล่าปลาหมึก

INGREDIENTS

300 grams fresh squid
2 tbsp. finely sliced hot chilli
3 tbsp. finely sliced shallot
3 tbsp. finely sliced lemon grass
1 tsp. finely sliced kaffir lime leaf
3 tbsp. fish sauce
3 1/2 tbsp. lime juice

PREPARATION

1. Remove the inedible portions of the squid, wash well, score the flesh in a fish-scale pattern, and cut into pieces one inch wide and two inches long.

2. Immerse the squid in boiling water until done, and then drain.

3. Mix the fish sauce and lime juice together, add the lemon grass, shallot, kaffir lime leaf and chillies and stir very gently to avoid bruising, Add the squid, work it around gently in the sauce, and then put the squid and sauce up on to a plate.

เครื่องปรุง

ปลาหมึกสด 300 กรัม
พริกขี้หนูซอย 2 ช้อนโต๊ะ
หอมแดงซอย 3 ช้อนโต๊ะ
ตะไคร้ซอย 3 ช้อนโต๊ะ
ใบมะกรูดซอย 1 ช้อนชา
น้ำปลา 3 ช้อนโต๊ะ
น้ำมะนาว 3 1/2 ช้อนโต๊ะ

วิธีทำ

1. ปลาหมึกเอาส่วนที่รับประทานไม่ได้ออก ล้างให้สะอาด บั้งเป็นเกล็ดปลา หั่นชิ้นกว้าง 1 นิ้ว ยาว 2 นิ้ว

2. ใส่น้ำลงในหม้อ ตั้งไฟ ใช้ไฟแรง พอน้ำเดือด ใส่ปลาหมึกลงลวกพอสุก เทน้ำออกให้สะเด็ด

3. ใส่น้ำปลา น้ำมะนาว คนให้เข้ากัน จึงใส่ตะไคร้ หอมแดง ใบมะกรูด พริกขี้หนู คนเบาๆ ผักจะได้ไม่ช้ำ ตักใส่จาน

PLA KAPHONG KHAO NEUNG PHRIK MA-NAO
Steamed sea perch with chillies in lime sauce
ปลากะพงขาวนึ่งพริกมะนาว

INGREDIENTS

1 sea perch weighing about 500 grams
6 peeled garlic cloves
5 sliced hot chillies
3 tbsp. lime juice
1 cup chicken stock
1 1/2 tbsp. light soy sauce

PREPARATION

1. Scale, clean, and wash the fish. With a knife, score the flesh along the length of the fish; then, place it in a deep bowl.

2. Chop the chillies and mix them with the chicken stock, lime juice, and soy sauce. The dominant taste should be sour.

3. Pour the mixture over the fish and place the pickled garlic on top.

4. After the water has begun boiling, place the fish in a steamer and steam over high heat for about 15 minutes. Remove from the steamer and serve hot.

เครื่องปรุง

ปลากะพงขาว
น้ำหนักประมาณ 500 กรัม **1** ตัว
กระเทียม **6** กลีบ
พริกขี้หนูหั่น **5** เม็ด
น้ำมะนาว **3** ช้อนโต๊ะ
น้ำซุปไก่ **1** ถ้วย
ซีอิ๊วขาว **1 1/2** ช้อนโต๊ะ

วิธีทำ

1. ขอดเกล็ดปลา ผ่าท้องควักไส้ออก ล้างให้สะอาด ใช้มีดบั้งตัวปลาตามยาว ใส่ชามก้นลึก พักไว้

2. ผสมน้ำซุป พริกขี้หนู น้ำมะนาว ซีอิ๊วขาว เข้า ด้วยกัน ชิมดูให้มีรสเปรี้ยวนำ

3. ราดส่วนผสมลงบนตัวปลา โรยกระเทียม

4. นำไปนึ่งในน้ำเดือดไฟแรง ประมาณ 15 นาที ยกลง เสิร์ฟร้อนๆ

PLA MEUK NEUNG MA-NAO
Steamed squid with lime sauce
ปลาหมึกนึ่งมะนาว

INGREDIENTS

10 squids (about 500 grams)
1/4 cup finely chopped red and green tiny hot chilli
1/4 cup finely chopped peeled garlic
1 tsp. sugar
1/4 cup fish sauce
1/4 cup lime juice

PREPARATION

1. Wash the squid well after removing the inedible portions.
2. Place a steamer half filled with water on medium heat. When the water is boiling, steam the squid for between three and five minutes. Remove them from the steamer, cut into bite-sized pieces, and arrange these on a plate.
3. Put the fish sauce, lime juice, and sugar in a bowl, stir until the sugar has dissolved, add the garlic, chilli, and stir to mix everything together. Spoon this sauce over the squid and serve.

เครื่องปรุง

ปลาหมึก (น้ำหนัก 500 กรัม) 10 ตัว
พริกขี้หนูสวนเขียว แดง สับละเอียด 1/4 ถ้วย
กระเทียมปอกเปลือกสับละเอียด 1/4 ถ้วย
น้ำตาลทราย 1 ช้อนชา
น้ำปลา 1/4 ถ้วย
น้ำมะนาว 1/4 ถ้วย

วิธีทำ

1. ปลาหมึกเอาส่วนที่รับประทานไม่ได้ออก ล้างให้สะอาด
2. ตั้งลังถึงใส่น้ำ 1/2 ของก้นลังถึง ใช้ไฟกลาง พอเดือด นำปลาหมึกนึ่ง 3-5 นาที ยกลง เรียงใส่จาน หั่นเป็นชิ้นขนาดพอคำ
3. ใส่น้ำปลา น้ำมะนาว น้ำตาล ลงในถ้วย คนให้ละลาย ใส่กระเทียม พริกขี้หนู คนให้เข้ากัน ตักราดบนปลาหมึก เสิร์ฟ

KUNG NEUNG RAT PHRIK MA-NAO
Steamed prawns with chilli and lime sauce
กุ้งนึ่งราดพริกมะนาว

INGREDIENTS

500 grams white prawns

2 tbsp. chopped mature ginger

15 hot chillies

20 cloves of fresh garlic

1 tbsp. finely chopped coriander root

3 pickled garlic bulbs

3 tbsp. finely chopped shallot

4-5 tbsp. lime juice

3 tbsp. fish sauce

1/2 tsp. sugar

1 bitter gourd

เครื่องปรุง

กุ้งแชบ๊วย 500 กรัม

ขิงแก่สับ 2 ช้อนโต๊ะ

พริกขี้หนู 15 เม็ด

กระเทียมสด 20 กลีบ

รากผักชีสับละเอียด 1 ช้อนโต๊ะ

กระเทียมดอง 3 หัว

หอมแดงสับละเอียด 3 ช้อนโต๊ะ

น้ำมะนาว 4-5 ช้อนโต๊ะ

น้ำปลา 3 ช้อนโต๊ะ

น้ำตาลทราย 1/2 ช้อนชา

มะระจีน 1 ลูก

PREPARATION

1. Wash, shell, and vein the prawns, line up one next to the other on a plate, and place the ginger on top. Place in a steamer in which the water is already boiling and steam until done (about 5 minutes); then, remove.

2. Chop the chilli, fresh garlic, coriander root, pickled garlic, and shallot up together fine, season with the lime juice, fish sauce, and sugar; stir well. Taste and adjust as required, and then pour over the steamed prawns.

3. Wash the bitter gourd, cut in half lengthwise, remove the insides, then slice, scald in boiling water to soften, and serve with the prawns. Garnish with mint and coriander leaves.

วิธีทำ

1. แกะเปลือกกุ้ง ผ่าหลังชักเส้นดำออก จัดใส่จาน วางขิงสับลงบนตัวกุ้ง แล้วนำไปนึ่งประมาณ 5 นาที กุ้งสุก ยกลง

2. สับพริกขี้หนู กระเทียม รากผักชี กระเทียมดอง หอมแดง รวมกันให้ละเอียด ปรุงรสด้วยน้ำมะนาว น้ำปลา น้ำตาล คนให้เข้ากัน ชิมรสตามชอบ แล้ว นำไปราดลงบนตัวกุ้งที่นึ่งเสร็จแล้ว

3. รับประทานกับมะระจีนหั่น ลวกพอสุก วางรอบ ๆ จาน เสิร์ฟกับกุ้ง แต่งด้วยผักชี ใบสะระแหน่

MU MA-NAO
Boiled pork with lime sauce
หมูมะนาว

INGREDIENTS	เครื่องปรุง
200 grams pork tenderloin	หมูสันนอก 200 กรัม
3 lettuce leaves	ผักกาดหอม 3 ใบ
1 slice of green lime	มะนาวเขียว 1 ชิ้น
5 red hot chillies	พริกขี้หนูแดง 5 เม็ด
2 tbsp. peeled small garlic cloves	กระเทียมกลีบเล็กปอกเปลือก 2 ช้อนโต๊ะ
1 tbsp. sugar	น้ำตาลทราย 1 ช้อนโต๊ะ
3 tbsp. fish sauce	น้ำปลา 3 ช้อนโต๊ะ
3 tbsp. lime juice	น้ำมะนาว 3 ช้อนโต๊ะ

PREPARATION

1. Wash the pork, cut into slices about 1 cm. thick, broil until done, and then cut crosswise into thin slices.

2. Chop the chilli and garlic until well mashed, add the sugar, fish sauce, and lime juice, and stir to mix.

3. Place the pork on a bed of lettuce arranged on a plate, pour on the sauce from Step 2, garnish with the lime slices, and serve.

วิธีทำ

1. ล้างหมูให้สะอาด หั่นเป็นชิ้นหนาประมาณ 1 ซม. นำไปย่างให้สุก หั่นเป็นชิ้นบาง ๆ ตามขวาง

2. สับพริกขี้หนูกับกระเทียมให้ละเอียด ใส่น้ำตาล น้ำปลา น้ำมะนาว คนให้เข้ากัน

3. วิธีจัด รองผักกาดหอม เรียงหมูย่าง ราดด้วย น้ำยำที่ปรุงไว้ (ส่วนผสมข้อ 2) วางมะนาว เสิร์ฟ

YAM TAENG
Spicy shredded cucumber salad
ยำแตง

INGREDIENTS

7 cucumbers
1/4 cup ground dried shrimp
1/4 cup yard-long bean,
cut into thin sliced and crushed
1-2 tomatoes, sliced
1 tbsp. ground roasted peanuts

DRESSING INGREDIENTS

1 tsp. chopped chillies
2 tsp. palm sugar
2 tbsp. fish sauce
2 tbsp. lime juice

Mix all the dressing ingredients together

PREPARATION

1. Wash the cucumbers, and shred them, removing the seeds.
2. Toss the shredded cucumber, tomato, and yard-long bean, together with the dressing. Then, add the ground dried prawn and ground roasted peanuts and toss again.
3. Arrange on a plate, garnish with slices of red spur chilli, and serve.

เครื่องปรุง

แตงกวา 7 ลูก
กุ้งแห้งป่น 1/4 ถ้วย
ถั่วฝักยาวหั่นท่อนสั้นบุบ 1/4 ถ้วย
มะเขือเทศหั่นเสี้ยว 1-2 ลูก
ถั่วลิสงคั่วบุบพอแตก 1 ช้อนโต๊ะ

เครื่องปรุงน้ำยำ

พริกขี้หนูสับ 1 ช้อนชา
น้ำตาลปีบ 2 ช้อนชา
น้ำปลา 2 ช้อนโต๊ะ
น้ำมะนาว 2 ช้อนโต๊ะ
ผสมเครื่องปรุงทั้งหมดเข้าด้วยกัน

วิธีทำ

1. ล้างแตงกวา ขูดเนื้อแตงให้เป็นเส้น ๆ ไม่เอาเมล็ด พักไว้
2. เคล้าเนื้อแตงกวา มะเขือเทศ ถั่วฝักยาว กับน้ำยำ ให้ทั่ว ใส่กุ้งแห้ง ถั่วลิสง เคล้าอีกครั้ง
3. จัดใส่จาน แต่งหน้าด้วยพริกชี้ฟ้าแดงหั่นฝอย เสิร์ฟ

KUNG NEUNG KHAI ROD SEAP
Spicy and sour steamed egg
กุ้งนึ่งไข่รสแซบ

INGREDIENTS

200 grams white prawns
2 eggs, 1 tsp. chopped chillies
2 tbsp. coriander leaves
1 tbsp. chopped garlic
1 tsp. sugar
2 tbsp. fish sauce
2 tbsp. lime juice

PREPARATION

1. Wash, shell, remove the shells and the heads but leave the tail fins in place. Cut them open along the black, and remove the vein.

2. Put the chillies, garlic, lime juice, fish sauce, and sugar in a bowl and stir to mix, and set aside.

3. Break the eggs into a mixing bowl and beat just enough to break the yolks. Divide the beaten egg, putting some into each of several small bowls. After the water in the steamer on medium heat has begun boiling, put the eggs into the steamer. When the egg is almost done, put one prawn into each cup. When done, remove from the heat.

4. Pour some of the sauce from Step 2 into each cup, sprinkle with the coriander leaves, and serve.

เครื่องปรุง

กุ้งแชบ๊วย 200 กรัม
ไข่ไก่ 2 ฟอง
พริกขี้หนูสับ 1 ช้อนชา
ผักชีเด็ดเป็นใบ 2 ช้อนโต๊ะ
กระเทียมสับ 1 ช้อนโต๊ะ
น้ำตาลทราย 1 ช้อนชา
น้ำปลา 2 ช้อนโต๊ะ
น้ำมะนาว 2 ช้อนโต๊ะ

วิธีทำ

1. ล้างกุ้ง แกะเปลือก เด็ดหัวไว้หาง ผ่าหลังชักเส้นดำออก พักไว้

2. ผสมพริกขี้หนู กระเทียม น้ำมะนาว น้ำปลา น้ำ-ตาล เข้าด้วยกัน

3. ต่อยไข่ใส่ถ้วยตีพอแตก เทใส่ถ้วยเล็กแบ่งเป็นหลายถ้วย นำไปนึ่งไฟกลาง พอใกล้สุก ใส่กุ้งในแต่ละถ้วย นึ่งจนสุก ยกลง

4. ราดด้วยส่วนผสมข้อ 2 โรยผักชี เสิร์ฟ

PLA CHAWN YANG SAEP
Northeastern-style broiled serpent-head fish
ปลาช่อนย่างแซบ

INGREDIENTS

1   serpent-head fish weighing
about 700 grams
1   tbsp. finely sliced spring onion
1   tbsp. finely sliced eryngo
(phak chi farang)
1   tbsp. finely sliced shallot
2   tbsp. coarsely ground parched rice
1   tbsp. ground pan-roasted dried chilli
3 1/2   tbsp. fish sauce
3   tbsp. lime juice

PREPARATION

1. Scale, clean, and wash the fish, and carve both sides of the body. Broil over a low charcoal fire until golden outside and done inside. Put it on a plate, and set aside.

2. Stir the fish sauce and lime juice together, add the ground dried chilli, parched rice, spring onion, shallot and eryngo, and stir to mix everything together. Pour this sauce over the fish, garnish with lettuce and serve.

เครื่องปรุง

ปลาช่อนน้ำหนัก 700 กรัม 1 ตัว
ต้นหอมซอย 1 ช้อนโต๊ะ
ผักชีฝรั่งซอย 1 ช้อนโต๊ะ
หอมแดงซอย 1 ช้อนโต๊ะ
ข้าวคั่วโขลกหยาบ ๆ 2 ช้อนโต๊ะ
พริกป่น 1 ช้อนโต๊ะ
น้ำปลา 3 1/2 ช้อนโต๊ะ
น้ำมะนาว 3 ช้อนโต๊ะ

วิธีทำ

1. ขอดเกล็ดปลา ผ่าท้องควักไส้ออก ล้างให้สะอาด บั้งทั้งสองด้าน นำปลาไปย่างไฟอ่อนจนสุกเหลือง จัดใส่จาน พักไว้

2. ผสมน้ำปลา น้ำมะนาว คนให้เข้ากัน ใส่พริกป่น ข้าวคั่ว ต้นหอม หอมแดง ผักชีฝรั่ง คนพอเข้ากัน ราดบนปลา แต่งด้วยผักกาดหอม เสิร์ฟ

YAM PHRIK WAN

Spicy sweet pepper salad

ยำพริกหวาน

INGREDIENTS

1/2   cup slices of boiled pork

1/2   cup small pieces of dry-pan-fried prawn

1   cup long thin slices of sweet pepper

9   small red and green hot chillies, pounded

1/4   cup ground roasted peanuts

3   tbsp. crisp-fried shallot slices

3   tbsp. crisp-fried garlic slices

1   tbsp. sugar

2   tbsp. fish sauce

2   tbsp. lime juice

PREPARATION

1. Mix the sugar, fish sauce, lime juice, and chillies together.

2. Mix the pork, prawn, and sweet peppers in a bowl, add the dressing from Step 1, and toss. Add the fried shallot, fried garlic, roasted, peanuts and toss once again.

3. Arrange on a plate and serve.

เครื่องปรุง

เนื้อหมูต้มหั่นชิ้นบาง 1/2 ถ้วย

เนื้อกุ้งหั่นชิ้นเล็กรวนพอสุก 1/2 ถ้วย

พริกหวานหั่นเป็นเส้นยาว 1 ถ้วย

พริกขี้หนูสวนเขียว แดง โขลกละเอียด 9 เม็ด

ถั่วลิสงคั่วโขลกหยาบ 1/4 ถ้วย

หอมแดงซอยเจียว 3 ช้อนโต๊ะ

กระเทียมซอยเจียว 3 ช้อนโต๊ะ

น้ำตาลทราย 1 ช้อนโต๊ะ

น้ำปลา 2 ช้อนโต๊ะ

น้ำมะนาว 2 ช้อนโต๊ะ

วิธีทำ

1. ผสมน้ำตาล น้ำปลา น้ำมะนาว พริกขี้หนู เข้าด้วยกัน พักไว้

2. ผสมเนื้อหมู เนื้อกุ้ง พริกหวาน ลงในชาม ใส่ส่วนผสมข้อ 1 ลงคลุกให้เข้ากัน ใส่หอมแดงเจียว กระ-เทียมเจียว ถั่วลิสงคั่ว เคล้าพอเข้ากัน

3. จัดใส่จาน เสิร์ฟ

PHLA PLA KROB

Spicy roasted fish salad

พล่าปลากรอบ

INGREDIENTS	เครื่องปรุง
1 cup roasted fish meat	ปลากรอบแกะเอาแต่เนื้อ 1 ถ้วย
1/4 cup mint leaves	สะระแหน่เด็ดเป็นใบ 1/4 ถ้วย
1 tbsp. coriander leaves	ผักชีเด็ดเป็นใบ 1 ช้อนโต๊ะ
1 red spur chilli, cut into long thin slices	พริกชี้ฟ้าแดงหั่นเป็นเส้น 1 เม็ด
3 tbsp. finely sliced lemon grass	ตะไคร้ซอย 3 ช้อนโต๊ะ
3 disk-shaped slices of galangal	ข่าหั่นแว่น 3 แว่น
3 shallots, sliced thin	หอมแดงซอย 3 หัว
7 garlic cloves	กระเทียม 7 กลีบ
1 red spur chillies	พริกชี้ฟ้าแดง 1 เม็ด
1/2 tbsp. sugar	น้ำตาลทราย 1/2 ช้อนโต๊ะ
1 tbsp. fish sauce	น้ำปลา 1 ช้อนโต๊ะ
3 tbsp. lime juice	น้ำมะนาว 3 ช้อนโต๊ะ

PREPARATION

1. Pound the two red chillies, and garlic together, add lime juice, fish sauce, and stir to mix.

2. Pound galangal, squeeze, collect the juice.

3. Toss the lemon grass, shallot, fish, the red spur chilli slices, with the dressing from Step 1 and the galangal juice.

4. Transfer to a plate, garnish with mint and coriander leaves, and serve.

วิธีทำ

1. โขลกพริกชี้ฟ้าแดง กระเทียม เข้าด้วยกันให้ละ-เอียด ใส่น้ำมะนาว น้ำปลา น้ำตาล คนให้เข้ากันเป็นน้ำปรุงรส

2. โขลกข่าให้ละเอียด บีบเอาแต่น้ำ พักไว้

3. ผสมตะไคร้ หอมแดง ปลากรอบ พริกชี้ฟ้า น้ำปรุงรส น้ำข่า เข้าด้วยกัน

4. จัดใส่จาน โรยหน้าด้วยสะระแหน่ ผักชี เสิร์ฟ

YAM PHRIK CHI FA
Spicy spur chilli salad
ย่ำพริกชี้ฟ้า

INGREDIENTS

100 grams small pieces of boiled fresh prawn

100 grams thin slices of boiled lean pork

100 grams thin sliced of boiled pork belly

1/2 cup dried shrimp ground
by pounding in a mortar

1/2 cup scalded strips of spur chilli

1/2 cup coriander leaves

3 tbsp. parched shredded coconut

2 tbsp. crisp-fried shallot slices

2 tbsp. crisp-fried garlic slices

DRESSING INGREDIENTS

1/2 cup coconut cream

3 roasted shallots

1-1 1/2 tbsp. palm sugar

11 1/2 tbsp. fish sauce

4 tbsp. tamarind juice

PREPARATION

1. Mash the roasted shallots in a mortar and then mix with the palm sugar, fish sauce, tamarind juice, and coconut cream. Heat the dressing to boiling, and then remove it from the heat and set aside until cool.

2. Arrange the spur chilli on a bed of lettuce on a platter. Next, place the prawn and the slices of lean pork and pork belly on top. Sprinkle the meats with the shredded coconut and ground dried shrimp, and then pour the dressing over them. Finally, sprinkle the salad with the fried shallot and garlic slices and the coriander leaves and serve.

เครื่องปรุง

กุ้งสดต้มหั่นชิ้นเล็ก 100 กรัม

เนื้อหมูต้มสุกหั่นชิ้นบาง 100 กรัม

หมูสามชั้นต้มหั่นชิ้นบาง 100 กรัม

กุ้งแห้งโขลกป่น 1/2 ถ้วย

พริกชี้ฟ้าหั่นเป็นเส้นลวกพอสุก 1/2 ถ้วย

ผักชีเด็ดเป็นใบ 1/2 ถ้วย

มะพร้าวคั่ว 3 ช้อนโต๊ะ

หอมแดงซอยเจียว 2 ช้อนโต๊ะ

กระเทียมซอยเจียว 2 ช้อนโต๊ะ

เครื่องปรุงน้ำยำ

หัวกะทิ 1/2 ถ้วย

หอมแดงเผา 3 หัว

น้ำตาลปีบ 1-1 1/ 2 ช้อนโต๊ะ

น้ำปลา 1 1/2-2 ช้อนโต๊ะ

น้ำมะขามเปียก 4 ช้อนโต๊ะ

วิธีทำ

1. โขลกหอมแดงพอแหลก แล้วจึงผสมกับน้ำตาล น้ำปลา น้ำมะขามเปียก หัวกะทิ ตั้งไฟพอเดือด พักไว้ให้เย็น

2. จัดพริกชี้ฟ้าลงจานที่ปูด้วยผักกาดหอม วางเนื้อ กุ้งต้ม เนื้อหมู เนื้อหมูสามชั้น โรยด้วยมะพร้าวคั่ว กุ้งแห้ง ราดด้วยน้ำยำ โรยหน้าด้วยหอมแดงเจียว กระเทียมเจียว ผักชี เสิร์ฟ

SOM TAM MALAKOR
Papaya salad
ส้มตำมะละกอ

INGREDIENTS

1 peeled and shredded
green papaya (about 3 cups)
1/4 cup ground dried shrimp
1 dried chilli soaked in water
6 garlic cloves
7 pepper corns
1/4 cup lemon, cut into small cubes
3 tbsp. palm sugar
3 tbsp. fish sauce
2 tbsp. lemon juice
1 tbsp. tamarind juice
1 lettuce plant

PREPARATION

1. Gently crush shredded papaya in mortar with pestle.

2. Crush garlic, dried chilli, and pepper corns in mortar, mixing thoroughly.

3. Mix tamarind juice, fish sauce, and sugar in a pot and heat to a boil. Remove from heat, allow to cool, add lemon juice, and mix with chilli paste in mortar.

4. Add the crushed papaya, the dried shrimp, and the lemon cubes and mix thoroughly.

5. Spoon onto a plate. Garnish with red spur chilli. Serve with lettuce.

เครื่องปรุง

มะละกอดิบ 1 ลูก
ขูดหรือสับเป็นเส้นเล็ก ๆ 3 ถ้วย
กุ้งแห้งป่น 1/4 ถ้วย
พริกแห้งแช่น้ำ 1 เม็ด
กระเทียม 6 กลีบ
พริกไทย 7 เม็ด
มะนาวหั่นสี่เหลี่ยมเล็ก ๆ 1/4 ถ้วย
น้ำตาลปีบ 3 ช้อนโต๊ะ
น้ำปลา 3 ช้อนโต๊ะ
น้ำมะนาว 2 ช้อนโต๊ะ
น้ำมะขามเปียก 1 ช้อนโต๊ะ
ผักกาดหอม 1 ต้น

วิธีทำ

1. โขลกมะละกอเบา ๆพอช้ำ
2. โขลกกระเทียม พริกแห้ง พริกไทย ให้ละเอียด
3. ผสมน้ำมะขามเปียก น้ำปลา น้ำตาล ลงในหม้อ ตั้งไฟพอเดือด ยกลง ทิ้งไว้ให้เย็น ผสมน้ำมะนาว ละลายน้ำพริก (ส่วนผสมข้อ 2) กับน้ำปรุงรสเข้าด้วยกัน
4. ใส่คลุกกับมะละกอ ใส่กุ้งแห้ง มะนาวที่หั่นไว้ ชิม-รส
5. ตักใส่จาน แต่งด้วยพริกชี้ฟ้าแดง เสิร์ฟกับผัก-กาดหอม

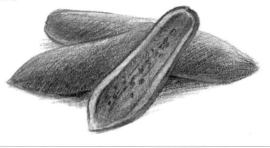

76

YAM PLA THU KAP SAI BUA

Spicy mackerel and water lily stem salad

ยำปลาทูกับสายบัว

INGREDIENTS

1 cup steamed mackerel meat
1 cup water lily stems cut diagonally into thin slices
9 chillies, crushed 1 tbsp. plam sugar
2 tbsp. fish sauce
2-3 tbsp. lime juice
Fresh vegetables : lettuce, mint leaves, shredded cabbage

PREPARATION

1. Mix the plam sugar, fish sauce, and lime juice together; then, add the chillies and set aside.

2. Toss the mackerel meat and water lily stems together. Add the dressing from Step 1 and toss gently. Transfer the salad onto a bed of lettuce arranged on a plate. And serve with fresh vegetables.

เครื่องปรุง

ปลาทูนึ่งแกะเอาแต่เนื้อ 1 ถ้วย
สายบัวซอยเฉียงบาง ๆ 1 ถ้วย
พริกขี้หนูสวนบุบพอแตก 9 เม็ด
น้ำตาลปีบ 1 ช้อนโต๊ะ
น้ำปลา 2 ช้อนโต๊ะ
น้ำมะนาว 2-3 ช้อนโต๊ะ
ผักสด : ผักกาดหอม สะระแหน่ กะหล่ำปลีซอย

วิธีทำ

1. ผสมน้ำตาลปีบ น้ำปลา น้ำมะนาว ให้เข้ากัน จึงใส่พริกขี้หนูลงผสม พักไว้

2. ผสมปลาทู สายบัว เข้าด้วยกัน แล้วจึงใส่ส่วนผสมข้อ 1 ลงคลุกเบา ๆ พอเข้ากัน จัดใส่จานที่รองด้วยผักกาดหอม เสิร์ฟพร้อมผักสด

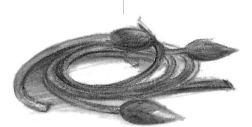

YAM PHRIK YUAK
Spicy bell chilli salad
ยำพริกหยวก

INGREDIENTS

10   bell chillies
100   grams shelled boiled white prawns
100   grams thin slices of boiled pork
1/4   cup coconut milk (100 grams grated coconut)
2   tbsp. crisp-fried shallot slices
2   tbsp. sugar
2   tbsp. fish sauce
2   tbsp. lime juice

PREPARATION

1. Roast the bell chillies. When done, cut them open, remove the seeds, and tear into long strips.
2. Heat the coconut milk until it boils and then remove it from the heat.
3. Mix the fish sauce, sugar, and lime juice together.
4. Toss the bell chilli, pork, prawn, coconut milk, and the dressing from Step 3 together. Taste and adjust the seasoning as desired.
5. Transfer the salad to a plate, sprinkle with the shallot, and serve.

เครื่องปรุง

พริกหยวก 10 เม็ด
กุ้งชีแฮ้ต้มแกะเปลือก 100 กรัม
เนื้อหมูต้มหั่นชิ้นบาง 100 กรัม
กะทิ (มะพร้าวขูด 100 กรัม) 1/4 ถ้วย
หอมแดงเจียว 2 ช้อนโต๊ะ
น้ำตาลทราย 2 ช้อนโต๊ะ
น้ำปลา 2 ช้อนโต๊ะ
น้ำมะนาว 2 ช้อนโต๊ะ

วิธีทำ

1. นำพริกหยวกไปเผาพอสุก แล้วผ่าเอาเมล็ดออก ฉีกเป็นชิ้นยาว ๆ
2. นำกะทิตั้งไฟพอเดือด ยกลง
3. ผสมน้ำปลา น้ำตาล น้ำมะนาว เข้าด้วยกันเป็น น้ำปรุงรส
4. เคล้าพริกหยวก เนื้อหมู เนื้อกุ้ง กะทิ น้ำปรุงรส เข้าด้วยกัน ชิมรส
5. ตักใส่จาน โรยหอมแดงเจียว เสิร์ฟ

YAM PLA CHAWN KROB
Spicy fried serpent-fish salad
ยำปลาช่อนกรอบ

INGREDIENTS

300　grams sliced serpent-head fish meat

1　tbsp. shreded young ginger

1-2　tbsp. finely sliced lemon grass

2　tsp. finely sliced kaffir lime leaves

2　tbsp. mint leaves

3　shallots, slices thin

2　tsp. ground pan-roasted dried chilli

1　tbsp. fish sauce

2　tbsp. lime juice oil for frying

PREPARATION

1. Place a wok on medium heat. When it is hot, pour in the oil, fry the fish golden brown, remove it from the oil, and set aside.
2. Add the lemon grass, young ginger, shallot, crisp-fried-fush, ground dried chillies, fish sauce, lime juice, mint and kaffir lime leaves toss once again.
3. Transfer on a plate and serve.

เครื่องปรุง

เนื้อปลาช่อนหั่นชิ้น　300　กรัม

ขิงอ่อนซอย　1　ช้อนโต๊ะ

ตะไคร้ซอย　1-2　ช้อนโต๊ะ

ใบมะกรูดซอย　2　ช้อนชา

สะระแหน่เด็ดเป็นใบ　2　ช้อนโต๊ะ

หอมแดงซอย　2　ช้อนโต๊ะ

พริกป่น　2　ช้อนชา

น้ำปลา　1　ช้อนโต๊ะ

น้ำมะนาว　2　ช้อนโต๊ะ

น้ำมันสำหรับทอด

วิธีทำ

1. ตั้งกระทะใช้ไฟกลาง พอร้อน ใส่น้ำมัน ทอดปลาให้กรอบ ตักขึ้น พักไว้
2. ใส่ตะไคร้ ขิง หอมแดง ปลาทอดกรอบ พริกป่น น้ำปลา น้ำมะนาว ใบมะกรูด ใบสะระแหน่ เคล้าพอทั่ว
3. จัดใส่จาน เสิร์ฟ

YAM NEUA ROD DED
Spicy broiled beef salad
ยำเนื้อรสเด็ด

INGREDIENTS

500	grams tender beef
15	chillies, sliced
2	tbsp. chopped garlic
1	bulb garlic, sliced
2	tsp. sugar
3	tbsp. fish sauce
3	tbsp. lime juice

PREPARATION

1. Wash the beef, broil over a medium charcoal fire until golden, brown, and then cut into slices.

2. In a bowl, toss the beef with the lime juice, fish sauce, and sugar toss to gently. Add the chillies. Pour the ingredients onto a bed of lettuce on a plate, and serve.

เครื่องปรุง

เนื้อสะโพก น้ำหนัก	500	กรัม 1	ชิ้น
พริกขี้หนูสวนซอย	15	เม็ด	
กระเทียมสับ	2	ช้อนโต๊ะ	
กระเทียมซอย	1	หัว	
น้ำตาลทราย	2	ช้อนชา	
น้ำปลา	3	ช้อนโต๊ะ	
น้ำมะนาว	3	ช้อนโต๊ะ	

วิธีทำ

1. ล้างเนื้อ นำไปย่างไฟแรงๆ และต้องคอยกลับเนื้ออย่าให้ไหม้ จนแห้งเหลือง จึงนำมาหั่นเป็นชิ้นบางๆ

2. ใส่เนื้อลงในชาม ใส่น้ำมะนาว น้ำปลา น้ำตาล เคล้าพอทั่ว แล้วจึงใส่พริกขี้หนู กระเทียม ตักใส่จานที่รองด้วยผักกาดแก้ว เสิร์ฟ

PHLA NEUA MA-KHEUA PRAW

Broiled beef and eggplant spicy salad

พล่าเนื้อมะเขือเปราะ

INGREDIENTS

300	grams beef sirloin
10	ma-kheua praw eggplants
1/4	cup mint leaves
2	tbsp. thinly sliced eryngo
	(phak chi-farang)
9	chillies, crushed
1/2	cup finely sliced lemon grass
1	tsp. sugar
3	tbsp. fish sauce
2	tbsp. lime juice

PREPARATION

1. Clean the beef, wrap in in foil or banana leaf and tie securely. Grill the beef over a low fire, and done. Cut it into bite-sized slice.

2. Mix the fish sauce, lime juice, sugar, and chillies.

3. Toss together the grilled beef and the dressing from Step 2.

4. Wash the eggplants, cut top to bottom into thin wedge-shaped sliced, and soak briefly in salt water to prevent their darkening.

5. Add the eggplants, lemon grass, and eryngo to the beef, toss to mix thoroughly, and then sprinkle with the mint leaves.

6. Transfer to a plate and serve.

เครื่องปรุง

เนื้อวัวสันใน 300 กรัม

มะเขือเปราะ 10 ลูก

สะระแหน่เด็ดเป็นใบ 1/4 ถ้วย

ผักชีฝรั่งหั่นฝอย 2 ช้อนโต๊ะ

พริกขี้หนูบุบ 9 เม็ด

ตะไคร้ซอย 1/2 ถ้วย

น้ำตาลทราย 1 ช้อนชา

น้ำปลา 3 ช้อนโต๊ะ

น้ำมะนาว 2 ช้อนโต๊ะ

วิธีทำ

1. ล้างเนื้อวัว ห่อด้วยใบตอง ย่างพอสุก นำมาหั่นชิ้นบางพอคำ

2. ผสมน้ำปลา น้ำมะนาว น้ำตาล พริกขี้หนู เข้าด้วยกัน

3. เคล้าเนื้อย่างและน้ำปรุง (ส่วนผสมข้อ 2) ไว้สักครู่

4. ล้างมะเขือเปราะ แล้วหั่นเสี้ยวบางๆ แช่ลงในน้ำเกลือ เพื่อไม่ให้มะเขือดำ

5. ใส่มะเขือเปราะลงในเนื้อย่าง ใส่ตะไคร้ ผักชีฝรั่ง เคล้าพอทั่ว โรยใบสะระแหน่

6. จัดใส่จาน เสิร์ฟ

TAP WAN
Savory liver
ตับหวาน

INGREDIENTS

200 grams beef liver
1 tbsp. ground parched rice
1/2 cup mint leaves
9 ground parched dried chillies
3 shallots, sliced
1 tbsp. fish sauce
1 tbsp. lime juice
Fresh vegetables : yard-long beans,
cabbage, swamp cabbage

PREPARATION

1. Wash the beef liver and slice into bite-size pieces. Immerse them in boiling water for a short time until very slightly done, and then place them on a dish.
2. Toss the liver with the lime juice, fish sauce, shallot, ground chillies, and ground parched rice. Taste and adjust the seasoning as desired. Place on a serving dish, sprinkle with the mint leaves, and serve with fresh vegetables.

เครื่องปรุง

ตับวัว 200 กรัม
ข้าวคั่วป่น 1 ช้อนโต๊ะ
สะระแหน่เด็ดเป็นใบ 1/2 ถ้วย
พริกขี้หนูแห้งคั่วป่น 9 เม็ด
หอมแดงซอย 3 หัว
น้ำปลา 1 ช้อนโต๊ะ
น้ำมะนาว 1 ช้อนโต๊ะ
ผักสด : ถั่วฝักยาว กะหล่ำปลี ยอดผักบุ้งไทย

วิธีทำ

1. ล้างตับวัว หั่นชิ้นเล็กบาง ๆ คั่วให้สุก ๆดิบ ๆ ตักใส่จานพักไว้
2. เคล้าตับกับน้ำมะนาว น้ำปลา หอมแดง พริกขี้หนู-ป่น ข้าวคั่ว ชิมรส จัดใส่จาน โรยหน้าด้วยสะระแหน่ เสิร์ฟพร้อมผักสด

TOM YAM PLA CHAWN

Sour and spicy serpent-head fish soup

ต้มยำปลาช่อน

INGREDIENTS

1 serpent-head fish weighing about 300 grams
3 roasted shallots
1 tbsp. fish sauce
2 tbsp. lime juice
2 tbsp. tamarind juice
2 kaffir lime leaves, torn into pieces
1 lemon grass stalk, cut diagonally into 1/2-inch-thick slices
1 spring shallot, sliced coarsely
1 eryngo plant, sliced coarsely
5-6 crisp fried dried hot chillies
2 cups water

PREPARATION

1. Scale, clean, and wash the serpent-head, and cut across the body into 1/2-inch-thick sliced.

2. Put the water in a pot and bring to a boil. Put in the lemon grass, kaffir lime leaves and shallots. When it returns to a boil, put in fish. Season with the tamarind juice, lime juice and fish sauce.

3. Add the spring shallot, eryngo, and crisp fried dried not chilli, stir everything together and remove from the heat. Pour into a bowl.

เครื่องปรุง

ปลาช่อน น้ำหนัก 300 กรัม 1 ตัว
หอมแดงเผา 3 หัว
น้ำปลา 1 ช้อนโต๊ะ
น้ำมะนาว 2 ช้อนโต๊ะ
น้ำมะขามเปียก 2 ช้อนโต๊ะ
ใบมะกรูดฉีก 2 ใบ
ตะไคร้หั่นเฉียง 1 ต้น
ต้นหอมหั่นหยาบ 1 ต้น
ผักชีฝรั่งหั่นหยาบ 1 ต้น
พริกขี้หนูแห้งทอด 5-6 เม็ด
น้ำ 2 ถ้วย

วิธีทำ

1. ขอดเกล็ดปลาช่อน ผ่าท้อง ควักไส้ออก ล้างหั่น เป็นแว่นหนา 1/2 นิ้ว

2. ใส่น้ำลงในหม้อ ตั้งไฟพอเดือด ใส่ตะไคร้ ใบมะ-กรูด หอมแดง พอเดือดอีกครั้ง ใส่ปลา ปรุงรสด้วย น้ำมะขามเปียก น้ำมะนาว น้ำปลา

3. ใส่ต้นหอม ผักชีฝรั่ง พริกขี้หนูทอด คนพอทั่ว ยกลง ตักใส่ถ้วย

TOM YAM KHAI PLA
Sour and spicy fish roe soup
ต้มยำไข่ปลา

INGREDIENTS

200 grams fish roe
4 disk-shaped slices of galangal
2 lemon grass stalks, sliced and crushed
3 kaffir lime leaves, torn into pieces
4-5 hot chillies, crushed
1/4 cup holy basil leaves
2 tbsp. fish sauce
3-4 tbsp. lime juice
2 cups soup stock

PREPARATION

1. Wash the roe well, and then set aside to drain.

2. Heat the stock in a pot, put in the galangal, lemon grass, and kaffir lime leaves, and when it comes to a boil, add the roe.

3. Season with the fish sauce. When the soup returns to boiling and the roe is done, put in the lime juice, chillies, and basil and turn off the heat.

4. Pour out into a bowl, and serve hot.

เครื่องปรุง

ไข่ปลา 200 กรัม
ข่าหั่นแว่น 4 แว่น
ตะไคร้หั่นท่อนทุบ 2 ต้น
ใบมะกรูดฉีก 3 ใบ
พริกขี้หนูบุบ 4-5 เม็ด
กะเพราเด็ดเป็นใบ 1/4 ถ้วย
น้ำปลา 2 ช้อนโต๊ะ
น้ำมะนาว 3-4 ช้อนโต๊ะ
น้ำซุป 2 ถ้วย

วิธีทำ

1. ล้างไข่ปลา พักไว้ให้สะเด็ดน้ำ

2. ใส่น้ำซุปลงในหม้อ ยกขึ้นตั้งไฟ ใส่ข่า ตะไคร้ ใบมะกรูด พอเดือด ใส่ไข่ปลา

3. ปรุงรสด้วยน้ำปลา เดือดอีกครั้งและไข่ปลาสุก ใส่น้ำมะนาว พริกขี้หนู กะเพรา ปิดไฟ

4. ตักใส่ชาม เสิร์ฟร้อนๆ

TOM YAM PLA KAO THOD KROB

Sour and spicy crisp grouper soup

ต้มยำปลาเก๋าทอดกรอบ

INGREDIENTS

1   grouper weighing 500-600 grams.
2   tbsp. eryngo (*phak chi farang*)
    cut into short pieces
1   rootlet of galangal, cut into slices
5   crushed lemon grass stems,
    cut into short pieces
5   kaffir lime leaves, torn into pieces
5   roasted dried chillies
1   tsp. ground dried chilli
3   tbsp. fish sauce
3-4   tbsp. tamarind juice
5   cups stock
    oil for frying

PREPARATION

1. Scale, clean, and wash the fish, score the flesh on either side attractively, and allow of drain.

2. Heat the oil in a frying pan on medium heat. When hot, fry the fish until crisp and golden; then, remove from the pan and drain.

3. Put the chicken stock in a pot, heat to boiling, and then add the galangal, lemon grass, kaffir lime leaves. Heat to a boil again, and add the grouper

4. Season to taste with the fish sauce, tamarind juice, and ground chilli. Tear the roasted dried chillies into pieces and add them to the pot. Then remove from the heat.

5. Transfer to a bowl, sprinkle with the eryngo, and serve.

เครื่องปรุง

ปลาเก๋า น้ำหนัก 500-600 กรัม 1 ตัว
ผักชีฝรั่งหั่นท่อนสั้น 2 ช้อนโต๊ะ
ข่าแก่หั่นท่อน 1 แง่ง
ตะไคร้ทุบหั่นท่อน 5 ต้น
ใบมะกรูดฉีก 5 ใบ
พริกแห้งเผา 5 เม็ด
พริกป่น 1 ช้อนชา
น้ำปลา 3 ช้อนโต๊ะ
น้ำมะขามเปียก 3 ช้อนโต๊ะ
น้ำซุป 5 ถ้วย
น้ำมันสำหรับทอด

วิธีทำ

1. ขอดเกล็ดปลา ผ่าท้องควักไส้ออก ล้างปลา บั้ง ทั้งสองด้าน พักไว้ให้สะเด็ดน้ำ

2. ใส่น้ำมันลงในกระทะ ตั้งไฟกลาง พอน้ำมันร้อน ใส่ปลาทอดให้เหลืองกรอบ ตักขึ้น พักไว้ให้สะเด็ด น้ำมัน

3. ใส่น้ำซุปลงในหม้อ ตั้งไฟ พอเดือดใส่ข่า ตะไคร้ ใบมะกรูด เดือดอีกครั้ง ใส่ปลาเก๋าทอดกรอบ

4. ปรุงรสด้วยน้ำปลา น้ำมะขามเปียก พริกป่น ชิมรส ฉีกพริกแห้งเผาใส่ ยกลง

5. ตักใส่ชาม โรยหน้าด้วยผักชีฝรั่ง เสิร์ฟร้อนๆ

TOM YAM KHA MU
Sour and spicy fresh pork hock soup
ต้มยำขาหมู

INGREDIENTS

1 kilogram Fresh pork hock
3 lemon grass stems
2 tbsp. coriander leaves
6 kaffir lime leaves
6 red spur chillies, sliced
2 tbsp. lime juice
3 tbsp. fish sauce
5 cups water

PREPARATION

1. Singe the hock over a fire until the skin turns yellow. Scrape with a knife to remove any hair. Wash, and then cut into diskshaped slices.

2. Pour the water into a pot. Pounded the lemon grass, slice into short lengths, and add to the pot. Tear the kaffir lime leaves into pieces and add to the pot. Put in the pork and place the pot over low heat. When the water boils, skim off the fat floating on the surface, simmer slowly until the pork is tender, and then remove from the heat. Be-careful not to over cook.

3. Put lime juice and fish sauce in a bowl with sliced spur chilli, pour the hot soup into the bowl, stir gently, taste and season additionally as you like, sprinkle with the coriander leaves and then serve right away.

เครื่องปรุง

ขาหมู (เลือกขาหน้า) 1 กิโลกรัม
ตะไคร้ 3 ต้น
ผักชีเด็ดเป็นใบ 2 ช้อนโต๊ะ
ใบมะกรูด 6 ใบ
พริกชี้ฟ้าแดงหั่นแฉลบ 6 เม็ด
น้ำมะนาว 2 ช้อนโต๊ะ
น้ำปลา 3 ช้อนโต๊ะ
น้ำ 5 ถ้วย

วิธีทำ

1. เอาขาหมูไปลนไฟจนเหลืองทั่ว ใช้มีดขูดขนออกให้หมด ล้างน้ำให้สะอาด หั่นเป็นแว่นๆ

2. ใส่น้ำลงในหม้อ ใส่ตะไคร้ทุบหั่นท่อนสั้น ใบ-มะกรูดฉีก ขาหมู ยกขึ้นตั้งไฟ ใช้ไฟอ่อน พอเดือดช้อนน้ำมันที่ลอยทิ้ง เคี่ยวไฟรุมๆ จนหนังหมูเปื่อยแต่อย่าให้เนื้อหมูเละ ยกลง

3. จัดเสิร์ฟโดยตักน้ำมะนาว น้ำปลา พริกชี้ฟ้า ใส่ถ้วย ตักขาหมูต้มร้อนๆใส่ คนเบาๆ ชิมรสตามชอบ โรยผักชี เสิร์ฟทันที

TOM PRIAO
Sour fish soup
ต้มเปรี้ยว

INGREDIENTS

1 sea perch weighing 500 grams
3 disk-shaped slices of ginger
2 disk-shaped slices of galangal
7 hot chillies, crushed
2 kaffir lime leaves, torn into pieces
2 lemon grass stalks, sliced and crushed
1 chopped coriander plant
3 shallots, crushed
2 tbsp. fish sauce
3-4 tbsp. tamarind juice
2 cups water

เครื่องปรุง

ปลากะพงขาว น้ำหนักประมาณ 500 กรัม 1 ตัว
ขิงหั่นแว่น 3 แว่น
ข่าหั่นแว่น 2 แว่น
พริกขี้หนูบุบ 7 เม็ด
ใบมะกรูดฉีก 2 ใบ
ตะไคร้หั่นท่อนทุบ 2 ต้น
ผักชีหั่น 1 ต้น
หอมแดงบุบ 3 หัว
น้ำปลา 2 ช้อนโต๊ะ
น้ำมะขามเปียก 3-4 ช้อนโต๊ะ
น้ำ 2 ถ้วย

PREPARATION

1. Scale, clean, and wash the fish, and then set aside to drain.

2. Put the water in a pot, and bring it to a boil. Put in the lemon grass, ginger, galangal, and shallots, and then the fish.

3. Season with the fish sauce, and tamarind juice. When the pot returns to boiling and the fish is done, add the hot chilli and kaffir lime leaves. Taste and adjust as required, and then turn off the heat.

4. Pour into a bowl, sprinkle with the coriander and serve hot.

วิธีทำ

1. ขอดเกล็ดปลา ผ่าท้องควักไส้ออก ล้างให้สะอาด พักไว้ให้สะเด็ดน้ำ

2. ใส่น้ำลงในหม้อ ตั้งไฟให้เดือด ใส่ตะไคร้ ขิง ข่า หอมแดง ใส่ปลา

3. ปรุงรสด้วยน้ำปลา น้ำมะขามเปียก เดือดอีกครั้ง และปลาสุก ใส่พริกขี้หนู ใบมะกรูด ชิมรส ปิดไฟ

4. ตักใส่ชาม โรยด้วยผักชี เสิร์ฟร้อนๆ

TOM YAM HUA PLA NAM SAI

Clear spicy fish head soup

ต้มยำหัวปลาน้ำใส

INGREDIENTS

1 red snapper head
2 tomatoes, cut into wedges
2 spring shallots, cut into 1 1/2-inch lengths
3 dried large chillies, cut into sections and fried crisp
5 pepper corns, pounded to break
5 slices peeled young galangal
1 lemon grass stalk, sliced diagonally
5 kaffir lime leaves, torn into pieces
1/4 cup fish sauce, 3 tbsp. lime juice
8 cups soup stock

PREPARATION

1. Wash the snapper head well and chop it into sections.

2. Put the eight cupfuls of water in a pot on high heat. When it comes to a boil, add the fish head and boil for ten minutes; then, pour off the water, and drain the fish head.

3. Pour the stock into a pot, and place on medium heat. When it boils, put in the galangal. When you can smell the fragrance of the galangal, add first the tomatoes and pepper and then the fish head, lemon grass, and kaffir lime leaves.

4. Season with the fish sauce and lime juice, adjusting as desired. Add the spring shallots and dried large chillies, pour into a bowl, and serve.

เครื่องปรุง

หัวปลากะพงแดง 1 หัว
มะเขือเทศหั่นชิ้น 2 ลูก
ต้นหอมหั่นท่อนยาว ขนาด 1 1/2 นิ้ว 2 ต้น
พริกแห้งหั่นท่อนทอดกรอบ 3 เม็ด
พริกไทยเม็ดทุบพอแตก 5 เม็ด
ข่าอ่อนปอกเปลือกหั่นแว่น 5 ชิ้น
ตะไคร้หั่นเฉียง 1 ต้น
ใบมะกรูดฉีก 5 ใบ
น้ำปลา 1/4 ถ้วย
น้ำมะนาว 3 ช้อนโต๊ะ
น้ำซุป 8 ถ้วย

วิธีทำ

1. ล้างหัวปลาให้สะอาด สับเป็นส่วนๆ

2. ใส่น้ำลงในหม้อ ตั้งไฟแรง พอน้ำเดือดใส่ปลาต้ม 10 นาที เทน้ำออก พักไว้ให้สะเด็ดน้ำ

3. ใส่น้ำซุปลงในหม้อ ตั้งไฟกลาง พอน้ำเดือดใส่ข่า พอหอมข่า ใส่มะเขือเทศ พริกไทย ปลาที่ต้ม ตะไคร้ ใบมะกรูด

4. ปรุงรสด้วยน้ำปลา น้ำมะนาว ชิมรส ใส่ต้นหอม พริกแห้ง ตักใส่ถ้วย เสิร์ฟ

KAENG SOM PLA CHAWN KROB
Sour tamarind soup with fried serpent-head fish
แกงส้มปลาช่อนกรอบ

INGREDIENTS

100　grams serpent-head fish meat
1/2　cup pieces of Chinese radish, carved to look like flowers
1/4　cup pieces of carrot, carved to look like flowers
1　cup slices cauliflower florets
1/2　cup lengths of yard-long bean
2　tbsp. sour soup curry paste
1　tbsp. sugar, 3　tbsp. fish sauce
3　tbsp. tamarind juice
4　cups water, oil for deep frying

INGREDIENTS FOR CHILLI PASTE

5　dried large chillies, seeds removed and soaked in water to soften
50　grams boiled serpent-head fish meat (without skin), 5　shallots
1/2　tsp. salt, 1/2　tsp. shrimp paste
Pound or blend all ingredient until ground

PREPARATION

1. Place a wok on medium heat. When it is hot, pour in the oil, fry the fish golden brown, remove it from the oil, and set aside.
2. Put the water in a pot, and place on medium heat. When it boils, add the curry paste, stir to disperse it, and then add the radish, carrot, and cauliflower and boil for about five minutes, until they are done.
3. Season with the fish sauce, tamarind juice, and sugar. When the soup returns to a boil, put in the yard-long beans and fried fish, simmer for two minutes. and then remove from the heat.

เครื่องปรุง

เนื้อปลาช่อน 100 กรัม
หัวไชเท้าจักเป็นดอก 1/2 ถ้วย
แครอทจักเป็นดอก 1/4 ถ้วย
กะหล่ำดอกหั่น 1 ถ้วย
ถั่วฝักยาวหั่นท่อน 1/2 ถ้วย
น้ำพริกแกงส้ม 2 ช้อนโต๊ะ
น้ำตาลทราย 1 ช้อนโต๊ะ
น้ำปลา 3 ช้อนโต๊ะ
น้ำมะขามเปียก 3 ช้อนโต๊ะ
น้ำ 4 ถ้วย
น้ำมันสำหรับทอด

เครื่องแกง

พริกแห้งแกะเม็ดออกแช่น้ำพอนุ่ม 5 เม็ด
เนื้อปลาช่อนต้มสุก 50 กรัม
หอมแดง 5 หัว
เกลือป่น 1/2 ช้อนชา
กะปิ 1/2 ช้อนชา
โขลกเครื่องแกงทั้งหมดเข้าด้วยกันให้ละเอียด

วิธีทำ

1. ตั้งกระทะใช้ไฟกลาง พอร้อน ใส่น้ำมัน ทอดปลาให้กรอบ ตักขึ้น พักไว้
2. ใส่น้ำลงในหม้อ ตั้งไฟ ใช้ไฟกลาง เมื่อเดือด ใส่น้ำพริกแกงส้มคนให้ละลาย ใส่หัวไชเท้า แครอท กะหล่ำดอก ต้ม 5 นาที จนสุก
3. ปรุงรสด้วยน้ำปลา น้ำมะขามเปียก น้ำตาล เดือดอีกครั้ง ใส่ถั่วฝักยาว ปลาช่อนทอด เคี่ยวต่อ 2 นาที ยกลง